INSIGHT COMPACT GUIDES

THE WEST OF IRELAND

GREAT · LITTLE · GUIDES

Compact Guide: The West of Ireland is the ideal quick-reference guide to this romantic, ethereal region. It tells you all you need to know about the West's attractions, from the down-to-earth delights of towns like Sligo and Galway to the splendid scenery of Connemara and the Burren, from thriving Celtic traditions to the haunts of W. B. Yeats.

This is one of almost 100 titles in *Insight Guides'* series of pocket-sized, easy-to-use guidebooks intended for the independent-minded traveller. *Compact Guides* are in essence travel encyclopedias in miniature, designed to be comprehensiv
date and authoritati

GW00703340

Star Attractions

An instant reference to some of the West of Ireland's's top attractions to help you set your priorities.

Craggaunowen Project p15

Glin Castle p18

Cliffs of Moher p22

Doolin p22

The Burren p23

Galway City p24

Aran Islands p27

Doo Lough p38

Croagh Patrick p40

Céide Fields p47

Famine Museum p59

THE WEST OF IRELAND

Introduction

Places

Culture

Leisure

Practical Information

West of Ireland – Europe's Western Shore

The West of Ireland is as much a state of mind as a geographical location. The Atlantic coastline of Ireland is the most westerly shore of Europe, the last mass of land before America. For both the Irish and their visitors, the West of Ireland, however vague its geographic definition, is the most distinctively Irish part of the country, the least influenced by English and European ways. Irish people see the West as a kind of idealised repository of Irish identity, the epitome of all that is special about Irishness, from the stone walls to the traditional music and dance.

Music festival in Ballina

It is also the least populated part of the country, its rugged scenery offering an isolation seldom experienced in more frequented parts of Europe. Everybody takes away their own favourite image of the West of Ireland: long summer evenings and twilit nights where darkness never quite falls; sheep grazing placidly in a stone-walled field; distant blue hills; sparkling lakes; mountain slopes ablaze with purple heather; deserted sandy beaches; clouds drifting in from the Atlantic bringing light showers of soft rain; the sound of a lark singing high above a headland; a curl of turf smoke rising from the roof of a low white cottage; the welcoming buzz of conversation; a sudden peal of music; the solemn ritual of the slow pouring of a pint of stout.

5

Geographical area

Travellers always know that they have reached the West when they see the first dry stone walls marching across hummocky green fields. There is a natural sweep from the shores of the River Shannon and its long sea estuary northwards up the coast to County Sligo, which includes most of the westerly extremities of Ireland's Atlantic coast. The rolling green farmland of the Shannon estuary and east County Clare is replaced by the grey rocks of the Burren which extend to the Aran Islands out in Galway Bay.

Dry stone walls and green fields

Galway, Mayo and Sligo all belong to the ancient Irish province of Connacht. Galway City is a thriving university town with a lively, cosmopolitan atmosphere. West of the city, in Connemara, the landscape changes to a combination of blanket bog and rock with the Twelve Ben Mountains to the north, and an intricately indented coastline to the south. This is the heart of the West, where the constantly changing weather has dramatic effects on the landscape, bathing it one minute in golden sunshine and the next minute hiding it under a cloud of grey mist. Visitors quickly learn not to despair at the first sign of rain: the weather changes in this part of the world as quickly as the clouds roll in from the Atlantic and away again.

Achill Island

Pastoral landscape in Clare

Burren blooms

Between Leenane and Westport the heather-clad hills of Connemara give way to a barer, more majestic landscape, dominated by the conical slope of Croagh Patrick. North of Westport lies Achill Island, whose particular combination of sheltered, fuchsia-lined lanes and wild Atlantic cliffs has stolen many a visitors' heart. Erris is a famously empty stretch of blanket bog which leads to the Mullet peninsula, a wild and beautiful place with many unfrequented beaches. On the cliffs of north County Mayo the Céide Fields is a huge Stone Age site whose field pattern was preserved for 5,000 years under a blanket bog.

After the wide open spaces of north County Mayo, the far smaller county of Sligo seems positively cosy. Its attractions, which include beaches whose rocks and sand abound in shells and fossils, and numerous megalithic graves, are all within easy reach. Visitors quickly understand why the poet W.B. Yeats and his painter brother Jack found so much inspiration in the area.

Geology and vegetation

The lands around the Shannon estuary in Kerry, Limerick and east Clare are limestone meadows, famous for their rich grasslands, where cattle, sheep and racehorses are raised. On the higher ground grassland is replaced by heather and gorse moors, interspersed with neat plantations of conifers. A sudden contrast to this pleasantly modulated landscape appears with the ghostly grey Burren in northwest Clare. Huge pavements of grey limestone dotted with massive boulders stretch as far as the eye can see. But look closely at the fissures of the rocks, and an unusually large range of wild flowers – Mediterranean, Arctic and Alpine – will be found growing side by side.

The west of counties Galway and Mayo is a complicated mixture of granite, quartzite and igneous rock intrusions. This contributes to the area's wild and varied landscape, dotted with many lakes. The scouring and moulding by the great glaciers of the Ice Age created the drowned valley of Killary Harbour on the Galway-Mayo border. The dramatic Atlantic coastline has steep cliffs and deep fjord-like inlets alternating with coastal lowlands fringed by sandy bays and offshore islands. Heavily glaciated, even the low-lying portions of Connemara and west Mayo have been stripped of soil. The barren rock surfaces hold innumerable lakes and bog patches. Movement of ice also affected the shape of the Sligo landscape. The valleys of Glencar and Sligo were eroded by the movement of ice, which picked up large amounts of sand and gravel which were laid down in big ridges from the Bricklieves to Ballysadare Bay. Hollows in the ground formed by the movement of the ice glacier were filled with water when the ice melted, forming numerous loughs.

Climate

The climate of the West of Ireland is largely the product of a westerly atmospheric circulation and the proximity of the Atlantic Ocean. The result is mild, damp weather, and a narrow temperature range – an average winter low of about 9°C (49°F) and an average summer high of about 54°C (68°F). There is no avoiding the fact that it rains a lot in the West of Ireland, but on the plus side, it is unlikely to be cold rain, and it can disappear as quickly as it started. Avoid the West between November and March. The driest period of the year is between April to June. May is the sunniest month with an average of 6–7 hours a day. The Burren receives 1,250–1,500mm (50–60 ins) of rain a year, while in Connemara there can be 2,000–3,000mm (80–120 ins) in the mountains, with less on the coast. Compare this to the east coast of Ireland which averages 760mm (30 ins) of rain per year, and you will see that, even by Irish standards, the West is wet.

Clouds over Connemara

7

Sunny day near Letterfrack

Celtic heritage

The first Celts arrived in Ireland from the continent of Europe in the Iron Age, around 300BC. Celtic Ireland was a hierarchical society, much given to tribal warfare, whose chief currency was cattle.

The Celts did not live in towns or villages, but rather in scattered farmsteads. Ireland, unlike the neighbouring British Isles, was never conquered by Rome, and the Celtic world order survived the arrival of Christianity in the mid-5th century. From the 12th century on, the east, the southwest and the north of the country were all influenced by either Norman, Scots or English settlers. However, the West, with the exception of the walled town of Galway, remained purely Celtic and Irish in language and social organisation. The apparently inhospitable nature of the landscape was partly responsible for this. Oliver Cromwell

Pub sign in Louisburgh

Achill Island local

Growing up on Clare Island

Flying the flag

thought so little of the West that he gave those Irish chieftains whose land he had confiscated the choice of going 'to Hell or Connacht'. As a result, there was an influx of people to the West of Ireland committed to the old ways of life as late as the mid-17th century.

The chief evidence of Celtic heritage today lies in the continued preference for scattered rural settlement over English-style towns and villages, which is especially evident in the sparsely populated areas of Connemara and Mayo, and in the survival of the language (now normally called Irish rather than Gaelic). The Aran Islands and South Connemara are two of the most important Irish-speaking areas (known as *Gaeltachts*) in the country, while University College Galway is an internationally recognised centre for the study of Celtic languages. While everyone living in these areas is bilingual, Irish is the chosen language of everyday life. Only about 56,500 Irish speakers live in Gaeltacht areas (the others are in Donegal, Kerry, Waterford and Cork), but just under 1.1 million Irish people claim the ability to speak the language.

Ever since the establishment of the Irish Free State in 1922, Irish has been the first language of the country, and the government has committed large sums of money to fostering it, most recently with the establishment of an Irish-language television station in Spiddal near Galway City. All children in state-supported schools must learn Irish, and must spend at least one summer break in a *Gaeltacht* area. Such an investment may seem anachronistic in this day and age, but there is more to Irish than just a minority language of historic interest.

It is not only the Irish language that survives in Ireland's *Gaeltacht* areas, but a whole culture, with its roots still fixed in the Celtic and Gaelic past. There is a palpably different way of life that goes with the Irish language which includes old forms of hospitality, and the persistence of old forms of entertainment such as recitations, story-telling and of course traditional music and dance. This, if you like, is the heart of the language, and the real purpose behind all the Irish language shop signs and signposts.

Economy and tourism

Visitors to the West often wonder how small farmers with perhaps twenty five acres of rocky land manage to make a living. The answer is with difficulty, and with much help from government grants and EU subsidies. The farmers are fortunate in that they own their own homes and the land around them, but such small plots are no longer enough to support a family. Most farmers and their spouses have a second job which could be anything from fishing to shift work in a high-tech factory, or seasonal work within the tourist industry.

The West has traditionally been an economically deprived area, due to the poor quality of the land. Sheep farming is the main occupation today with small-scale cattle raising and dairy farming on the better land. The only period when population grew significantly was the early 19th century, when large families living on potatoes could subsist on as little as one acre of fertile ground. When the potato crop failed between 1845–48, about 1.4 million people died and the same amount again emigrated. The West of Ireland was one of the worst affected regions, and took years to recover. Up until the 1970s, the West was a sad and empty place, with the only option for many people being emigration to menial jobs in the UK or America. Nowadays the farmers' children probably have university degrees and, if they are lucky, a good job in Galway or Dublin.

Tourism has had a beneficial influence on the area and has been a major factor in the region's recovery from economic depression (the other has been investment in high-tech industries encouraged by government grants). Large country houses that might otherwise have fallen into ruin have been successfully converted into luxury hotels. It is well worth visiting historic places like Ashford Castle or Ballynahinch Castle for coffee or bar food or dinner simply to savour the atmosphere. Like the rest of the West of Ireland, these are largely informal places where nobody stands on ceremony.

Many a family's economy has been boosted by the Bed and Breakfast business. Whatever your budget, it is worth trying a few B&Bs to sample Irish hospitality at its simplest but often its best. Traditionally, the West has been a destination for people who enjoy the outdoor life, offering superb facilities for anglers, golfers, walkers, climbers and horse-back riders. The growth in tourism has led to more investment in all-weather facilities, particularly heritage centres. Projects like the Strokestown Famine Museum, have increased awareness and understanding of Ireland's complex history. And above all, the growth in visitor numbers has finally led to the enforcement of litter and dumping laws, tidying up the region's farms and villages.

Landlady and her guests

But prosperity brings its own problems, and they are not limited to traffic gridlock in Galway City. Many visitors complain of the visual blight caused by house-building in inappropriate styles in areas of great scenic beauty. There are undeniably tensions in the West between environmentalists and developers, but people are aware of this problem, and are actively seeking a solution which allows sustainable development without spoiling the natural, unpolluted landscape that attracts so many visitors to the area in the first place.

Away from it all in Co. Galway

Historical Highlights

7000BC Earliest hunter settlers arrive across the narrow waters between Britain and Ireland.

5,000BC The first Neolithic farmers arrive. They put down their roots, clear the land, raise cattle and till newly created fields. One such colony settled at Céide Fields in Co. Mayo.

1200BC More sophisticated people arrive, producing a greater variety of artefacts and constructing palisade lake dwellings on artificial islands. Elaborate megalithic burial tombs like the Poulnabourne dolmen in the Burren are introduced.

500BC Arrivals of Celtic people from central Europe. The Celts soon dominate Ireland.

200BC onwards Celtic Ireland is not unified politically – only by culture and language. The country is divided into about 150 miniature kingdoms, subject to a more powerful king, who is in turn subject to one of five provincial kings. The High King of Ireland rules from Tara in Co. Meath. Society is regulated by Brehon Laws, an elaborate code of legislation.

AD432 Christianity comes to Ireland. St Patrick becomes the Irish Apostle, preaching a new creed that is readily and widely embraced.

600-900 Regarded as the Golden Age. Christianity flourishes and gives rise to the establishment of monasteries, such as Ennis Friary, attended by scholars from all over Europe. In these monasteries the earliest illuminated manuscripts in Irish and Latin are written. Also a period of great artistic expression in precious metals, evidenced by the Cross of Cong, now in the National Museum in Dublin.

650 Saint Mac Dara founds a monastery on Mac Dara's Island off the Connemara coast.

800 Norse-Viking raids along the coast and striking inland along major rivers, plundering the treasure of the monasteries, including that on Innismurray island, Co. Sligo. Later, Vikings establish their own settlements and develop commerce and the first urban societies in Dublin, Cork, Limerick and Waterford.

1120 Cong Abbey, Co. Mayo, founded for the Augustinian Order.

1169 Normans land in Ireland and consolidate their hold with a network of castles and keeps.

1216 Ballintubber Abbey, Co. Mayo, founded by Cathal O'Connor, King of Connacht.

1235 Norman conquest of Mayo. Anglo-Norman de Burgos captures the fort on the Corrib estuary and replaces it with a formidable castle. The settlement around it grows into Galway City.

1252 Sligo Abbey founded by Norman baron, Maurice Fitzgerald, for the Dominican order.

1484 Galway's leading merchant families, later known as the Fourteen Tribes of Galway, elect their first Lord Mayor, a Lynch.

1541 Henry VIII declares himself King of Ireland, and relentlessly pursues his dissolution of the monasteries. English settlers introduced into the West, and military campaigns launched against troublesome Irish lords.

1570 Mayo County established.

1585 Iar-Connacht divided into four baronies by Elizabeth I's Lord Deputy. Three out of four local chieftains refuse to sign the deed.

1588 Spanish Armada ships wrecked all along the west coast.

1601 The English defeat the Irish and Spanish at the Battle of Kinsale. For the first time the entire country is run by a strong English central government, ruling from Dublin Castle.

1607 Native Irish lords of Ulster go into voluntary exile in the 'flight of the earls'. Settlers from England and the lowlands of Scotland introduce a different society to the rest of Ireland; building towns, establishing markets and trade and changing farming methods.

1611 Castlebar town granted charter by King James I. Sligo is created a municipal and parliamentary borough one year later.

1649 Oliver Cromwell lands in Ireland. Death for some, confiscation of property and banishment to Clare or Connacht for others. Connacht is finally conquered in 1653.

1690–2 William of Orange defeats the army of James II at the Battle of the Boyne. One year later the Jacobites are defeated again at Aughrim in Co. Galway. Following the Treaty of Limerick, Jacobite followers of Patrick Sarsfield leave to join the Catholic armies of Europe.

1730 Westport House built, one of the few important neoclassical buildings from this period in the West.

1749 Brian Merriman, last great poet of old Irish language bardic tradition, born in Ennistymon.

1798 French force lands at Killala Bay in support of Irish insurrection, later crushed.

1816 John D'Arcy founds the town of Clifden in an effort to lure the people away from their smuggling livelihood on the Connemara coast.

1818–35 Alexander Nimmo constructs a road link between Clifden and Galway. Harbours at Cleggan, Clifden, Roundstone and Rossaveale also built during these years.

1828 Daniel O'Connell returned as MP for Clare, thus initiating the chain of events that lead to Catholic Emancipation the following year.

1845 Potato crop fails and famine follows with crop failure again the next three years. Death and emigration reduces population by some 2 million.

1879 Religious apparition reported at Knock.

1880 Captain Boycott of Co. Mayo ostracised at harvest time and the word 'boycott' is coined.

1890 Congested Districts' Board established to promote development of traditional crafts and industries in the still over-populated West of Ireland. It lasts until 1920 when the new Irish government replaced it with *Gaeltarra Éireann*.

1892 Foxford Woollen Mills in Co.Mayo established by Agnes Morrogh-Bernard of the Sisters of Charity to relieve unemployment.

1893 Gaelic League founded.

1916 Easter Uprising put down within a week. Execution of its leaders unites the people.

1917 Eamon de Valera elected member of parliament for East Clare at Ennis.

1918 Sinn Féin win general election followed by the formation of the first Dáil or Independent Parliament, which in turn is followed by a guerrilla war with British forces.

1921 Anglo-Irish Treaty ends the war and Irish Free State formed. Six of the nine Ulster counties given their own parliament in Belfast within the United Kingdom. Civil war ensues in the South, ending in 1923 with the defeat of the Republican forces.

1923 W.B.Yeats, whose poetry reflects his love for Sligo, receives the Nobel Prize for Literature.

1945 Shannon International Airport opens.

1948 The Irish Free State declares itself a Republic and leaves the British Commonwealth.

1952 John Ford's *The Quiet Man*, starring John Wayne and Maureen O'Hara, filmed in colour in Cong, Co. Mayo.

1971 Population of the West of Ireland shows an increase for the first time since the 1840s.

1972 *Radio na Gaeltachta*, the Irish language radio station, begins broadcasting from Casla, Co. Galway.

1973 Ireland joins the European Economic Community (forerunner of the EU).

1976 Basilica opened close to the site of apparition in Knock in Co. Mayo.

1977 First Japanese manufacturing plant established near Killala, Co.Mayo.

1986 Knock Airport opens.

1993 Céide Fields archaeological centre opened at the site of the largest Stone Age farming excavations in Europe.

The Shannon at Limerick City

Route 1

Ennis and the Shannon Estuary

Ennis – Limerick city – Foynes – (Tarbert to Killimer ferry) – Kilrush – Carrigaholt – Kilbaha – Ennis (257km/160 miles) *See map, page 16*

This route starts from Ennis, the chief town of County Clare, and travels south through a region richly endowed with 14th, 15th- and 16th-century castles, both ruined and restored. Bunratty, mid-way between Shannon Airport and Limerick City, is one of Ireland's biggest castles, and is complemented by a lively Folk Park which brings rural Ireland of the turn of the century vividly to life. The route continues to Limerick, the Republic's third-largest city, whose attractions include the Hunt Museum, a unique collection of art and artefacts from all over Europe. Limerick is built on the magnificent River Shannon, at 273km (170 miles), the longest river in Ireland or Britain. The route follows the south bank of the Shannon estuary, visiting the Aviation Museum at Foynes which recalls the era of transatlantic flying boats, and a magnificent 18th-century stately home, Glin Castle. From Tarbert the route crosses the Shannon by car ferry, visiting Kilrush and Kilkee, pleasant seaside resorts.

Rural roots at Bunratty

Ennis is a quiet market town and the municipal capital of Co. Clare. A statue at its centre commemorates 'the Liberator', Daniel O'Connell, MP for Clare, whose oratory and political skill won Catholic Emancipation at Westminster in 1829. Eamon de Valera represented the people of Ennis in the Republic's parliament from 1917 to 1959, and is commemorated in a statue outside the clas-

Preceding pages: Dunguaire Castle near Kinvara

sical courthouse and in the **De Valera Library Museum**, Harmony Row (Monday and Thursday 11am–5.30pm, Tuesday, Wednesday and Friday 11am–8pm), a small museum with various items of historical interest. In spite of a one-way system there are still traffic jams, and the town's colourful but narrow streets are best explored on foot. Don't miss the remains of the 13th-century **Friary**. Just by the hump-backed bridge on the river Fergus, the cloistered friary was originally built by the Franciscans. In the 14th century it was home to 350 friars who taught over 600 students at its school, which was considered one of the best in Ireland. It was finally suppressed in 1692.

Craggaunowen Project: dwelling

Leave Ennis on the R469 for the village of **Quin**. Just before the village, a lane on the right leads to the ★★ **Craggaunowen Project** (Easter to October 10am–6pm, mid-May to August from 9am). A recreated lake-dwelling, a ring fort and an excavated Iron Age road give some idea of the lifestyle at the dawn of history. Also on display is *The Brendan,* a traditional currach built in leather and wood, in which explorer Tim Severin retraced St Brendan's 7th-century voyage to America.

In Quin itself, the ruins of the mid-15th century **Friary** include the cloisters and the tower. Climb to the first storey for a good view of the layout. They were built on top of a Norman castle dating from 1280, which in turn was built on the site of an earlier monastery.

Another 3km (2 miles) south is ★ **Knappogue Castle** (Easter to October 9.30am–5pm), a 16th-century tower house with massive walls. It has been extensively restored and lavishly furnished. The castle is now used for 'medieval' banquets, light-hearted entertainments with Irish cabaret which are extremely popular with first-time visitors (tel: 061-360788 for bookings).

Knappogue Castle

Head now for Sixmilebridge and join the R462 for Cratloe and the N18. It is almost impossible to miss the signs for ★★★ **Bunratty Castle & Folk Park** (castle daily 9.30–5.30pm, park to 6.30pm; last admission one hour before closing). Essentially a fortified home, the massive 15th-century castle was extensively restored in the 1960s and now contains a fine collection of furniture, tapestries and paintings from the 14th to 16th centuries. As at Knappogue, medieval banquets are held nightly in the main hall. (Same telephone number for bookings – *see above.*)

Bunratty Castle: the banquet hall

The park opens to a reconstructed 19th-century village. The forge, the post office, the farmhouse and the labourer's cottage are all 'inhabited' by the appropriate person, who may be baking bread or lighting the fire as you call by. Hens peck around outside the front doors. It's all very touristy, but even the most sophisticated visitor tends to get caught up in the charm of it all, while children love it. Before leaving Bunratty, stop for a break at Durty Nelly's, one of Ireland's most famous pubs.

Limerick City: Castle Street

The main N18 to **Limerick City** takes one over Sarsfield Bridge, with a view of the restored King John's Castle to the north. The castle is the historical centrepiece of a city of some 52,000 people. Vikings raided the early settlement in the 9th century, sailing their high-prowed boats up the Shannon estuary. But the Normans, who built the castle, made good use of the city's strong trading position on the River Shannon. As a walled city, Limerick was under siege over the centuries. In 1690, during the Williamite wars, the Irish leader Patrick Sarsfield slipped out of the city to ambush and destroy a vital munitions train being brought up by the besiegers. Two years later, however, another siege ended with the signing of the Treaty of Limerick. This Treaty, reputedly signed on a stone still to be seen on Thomond Bridge, was later broken by the victorious Williamites. The episode marked the exodus of the first Irish soldiers to leave Ireland and serve in the Catholic armies of Europe, the so-called Wild Geese.

One of many pubs in town

16

Oddly enough, Limerick has no known connection with the comic five-line rhyme form known as the limerick.

Until recently Limerick's city centre resolutely turned its back on its best asset, the River Shannon. New developments have concentrated on showcasing attractive stretches of river. One such modern building, at Arthur's Quay, houses the **Tourist Information Office**. The TIO organises walking tours of the city in the summer.

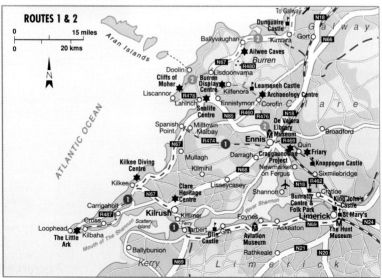

Head north of Arthur's Quay for **The Custom House** to view the ★★★ **The Hunt Museum** (Tuesday to Saturday 10am–5pm; Sunday 2pm–5pm) which contains a remarkable collection of antiquities from pre-Christian times onwards of Irish, Greek, Roman and Egyptian origin. Included here are a bronze horse by Leonardo da Vinci, a revered coin said to be one of the '30 pieces of silver' for which Christ was betrayed, and the crucifix worn by Mary Queen of Scots at her execution. This private collection was bequeathed to the nation by the Hunt family. It is exhibited on three floors of the renovated 18th-century Custom House.

The Hunt Museum

The old, chiefly Georgian part of Limerick will also be found to the north of Arthur's Quay. **St Mary's Cathedral** dates from the 12th century. Its most interesting feature is the black oak seats of its misericords which are carved with animal figures.

King John's Castle (mid-April to October 9.30am–5.30pm; November to mid-April noon–4pm) was built by the Normans in the 13th century. A recently added glass entrance hall spoils the first impressions of this imposing Anglo-Norman edifice. Climb one of its round towers for a good view of the town. An audiovisual display introduces Limerick's history.

St Mary's Cathedral

17

King John's Castle

Also worth a visit is the **Beltable Arts Centre** at 69 O'Connell Street which has contemporary exhibitions and a small theatre, and the small and under-funded but very pleasant **City Gallery** housed in a neoclassical building in **Pery Square** beside the **People's Park**, near the railway station. There is a small collection of Irish art and visiting contemporary exhibitions.

Leave Limerick on the N69 Askeaton road. This leg of the N69 rolls between hedgerows of good farming country, emerging at the Shannon estuary at **Foynes**. Nowadays Foynes is a busy working port. Sixty years ago it was a very different place, famous as the landing point of the first transatlantic air traffic. The romance of the era of the flying-boats is recaptured in the ★ **Aviation Museum** (April to October daily 9.30am–6pm). From 1937 until 1945 great flying-boats operating between America and Europe landed on the sheltered stretch of water between the mainland and Foynes Island. The museum contains the original radio and weather room with its transmitters and receivers and Morse code equipment. In spite of Ireland's neutrality in World War II, Foynes was a secret base for Allied Intelligence, quartered in the operations building.

Foynes was also the birthplace of Irish coffee. When an aircraft was forced by bad weather to return to Foynes, as often happened, the barman, Joe Sheridan, reckoned that the cold, frustrated passengers deserved a drop of whiskey and a large spoon of sugar in their coffee. Having no milk to hand, he dropped a dollop of whipped cream on top and discovered that it floated above the coffee in an uncanny imitation of a pint of stout. Sheridan's creation is celebrated annually in an Irish Coffee Festival at which bar staff compete to produce the perfect sample.

Views of the Shannon estuary come and go on your right as the road continues to Glin, and a fine stately home, ★★ **Glin Castle** (May and June 10am–noon, 2–4pm; other times by appointment, tel. 068/34173). Beautifully situated on the banks of the Shannon, the present building dates from 1785, although there has been a Fitzgerald castle on the site since the 14th century. It is the seat of the head of the Fitzgerald clan, the Knight of Glin. The crenelations were added in the early 19th century to make the house look more castle-like. Here you will find, among porcelain and pictures, an exceptional collection of Irish mahogany and walnut furniture. There is also delicate plasterwork and a breathtaking 'flying' staircase. Glin has been nominated as one of the world's outstanding private houses. The formal gardens and kitchen garden of the house are included in guided tours. Guests can stay at Glin for dinner, bed and breakfast by arrangement.

Glin Castle

18

A small car ferry operates across the Shannon estuary between Tarbert and Killimer, making the 20-minute crossing every hour on the half-hour during daylight hours. On a clear day you can see all the way down the Clare peninsula to Loop Head.

Head for ★ **Kilrush** on the N57. A pleasant, old fashioned town with wide streets, Kilrush was designed and built in the 18th century by the local landlord. Horse fairs are still held in its Market Square. The Market House is now the **Kilrush Heritage Centre** (May to September, Monday to Saturday 9.30am–5.30pm, Sunday noon–4pm) which illustrates the town's history. The **Scattery Island Visitor Centre** (mid-June to September, daily 9.30am–6.30pm) to the west of Merchant's Quay explains the history of **Scattery Island**, 3km (2 miles) offshore, whose 6th-century monastery was founded by St Senan. The ruins of five medieval churches are dominated by a 33-m (115ft) high round tower. Boats for the island leave from the **Kilrush Creek Marina** (tel: 065/51327).

Kilkee

Kilkee is a much smaller town, a seaside resort with accessible cliff walks, popular with residents of Limerick city and very busy during the summer. Kilkee was rated by Jacques Cousteau as among the best five diving locations in the world. The **Kilkee Diving Centre** (tel: 065/56707) provides services for both expert and novice.

Head south on the R487 and the R488 for Carrigaholt. **Dolphin-watch boats** leave from the pier on two-hour

Carrigaholt pier

cruises. An 80-strong school of bottlenose dolphins cruises in the area. (May to September; booking essential, tel: 065/584711.)

Return to the R487 and continue south. This is an exceptionally scenic stretch of road, but also a narrow and bumpy one, which runs down the sparsely inhabited peninsula that forms the northern extremity of the Shannon estuary, to the lighthouse at Loop Head. Huge Atlantic waves pound the cliff faces in stormy weather.

Along the R487

Kilbaha harbour village is just a little way from its local church, standing almost alone in **Moneen**. Here you find a touching reminder of Penal times when Catholics were denied civil and religious liberties. Inside the church there is ★ **The Little Ark** (daily 9am–6pm), a timber caravan which was wheeled out for Sunday Mass to the nearby foreshore. This was out of the jurisdiction of the local landlord who had refused permission for a church building. Over the church door a stained-glass window portrays the scene.

Return to Kilkee and choose between the N68, which takes a shorter but less scenic route to Ennis (56km/35 miles), or the N67 to Milltown Malbay and the R474 to Ennis (78km/48 miles). The longer route has an excellent stretch of sea views at **Spanish Point** between Quilty and Milltown Malbay. Sandy dunes rise up on your left, held together by clumps of machair grass. Long curving beaches are pounded by waves rolling in from the Atlantic. Spanish Point was named in memory of survivors of a wreck of the Spanish Armada who swam ashore here only to be executed by the High Sheriff of Clare. It is now a popular holiday spot, much frequented by surfers looking for the perfect Atlantic roller, while **Milltown Malbay** is famous for its traditional music summer school, The Willie Clancy Week, which is held every year in early July.

Fresh lobster

19

Atlantic rollers, Spanish Point

Route 2

The Burren and the Cliffs of Moher

Corofin – Kilfenora – Ennistymon – Lahinch – Liscannor – Cliffs of Moher – Doolin – Lisdoonvarna – Ballyvaughan (180km/110 miles) *See map on page 16*

The Burren

This route goes across country from Ennis via Corofin and Kilfenora to the spectacular Cliffs of Moher, which rise vertically out of the Atlantic. We then explore the area of exposed limestone known as the Burren, a rocky grey landscape dotted with enormous grey boulders, which is often compared to a moonscape. The Burren is an area of limestone pavements, and much of it consists of gently sloping hills which lead down to the sea, with views of the Aran Islands and Galway Bay. Man has lived and farmed here for over 5,000 years, and more than 100 prehistoric tombs and 500 ring forts remain. A close look at the cracks in the limestone pavements will reveal the unusual flora of the Burren: plants from both the Arctic and the Alps growing side by side, often underground.

Leave Ennis on the N85 Ennistymon–Lahinch road, turning right after about 4km (3 miles) onto the R476 Corofin–Kilfenora road. There are several optional stops on this route; if you take all of them you will end up something of an expert on the area. The **Dysert O'Dea Castle Archaeology Centre** (May to September daily 10am–6pm) is located in a 15th-century castle on the edge of the little village of **Corofin**. There are 25 ancient monuments within a mile's radius dating from the Bronze Age to the 19th-century, and they are all explained in a comprehensive introduction to the archaeology of the area.

Culture in Doolin

If Irish roots are of interest, seek out the **Clare Heritage Centre** (museum April to October daily 10am–6pm; November to March genealogy service only, Monday to Friday 9am–5pm) in Corofin's disused Protestant church. The Centre offers a genealogical service and also do-it-yourself advice. The museum has a display on the west of Ireland in the 19th century which proves as sobering introduction to an area that suffered more than most from famine and emigration. Before the great famine of 1845 the population of County Clare was 286,394. By 1891 famine and emigration had reduced the figure to 112,334. Nowadays it has stabilised at around 190,000.

Beyond Corofin you will get your first glimpse of the Burren as the land becomes more rocky, and grey replaces green as the dominant colour. The ruin of **Leamaneh Castle** can be seen to the right of the road, 8km (5 miles) west of Corofin. It is an imposing sight with its empty windows staring over the hills. Originally an O'Brien tower house dating from the late 15th century, it was expanded into a larger, four-storey house in the 17th century. The castle stands on private grounds; for permission to view ask at the modern house to the left of the castle.

21

Today ★ **Kilfenora** is a tiny village with a population of under 200, where the main event is a weekly sheep market held in its main street. However, Kilfenora was once a bishop's see, and has its own ruined 12th-century cathedral (freely accessible). Three medieval High Crosses carved with figures and ornaments stand around it. The historical background, and the geology and the flora and fauna of the area, is explained in the ★ **Burren Display Centre** (June to August 9am–7pm, mid-March to May and September to November 10am–4.30pm), a small, old fashioned but informative visitor centre.

Kilfenora's cathedral: detail

Burren Display Centre

Leave Kilfenora on the tiny R481, driving 8km (5 miles) south to visit **Ennistymon**, a charming, old fashioned resort town on the Cullenagh River which has retained many original wooden shop fronts. The river has a series of waterfalls visible from its seven-arched bridge.

From Ennistymon it is 4km (2½ miles) to the coast and **Lahinch**, a small resort with a long sandy beach backed by dunes, chiefly famous for its golf links. There are now two golf courses here. The more challenging is the old course, completed in 1892, which features numerous 'blind shots' in which your target is hidden by towering sand hills.

Golf at Lahinch

A sweep around Lahinch Bay on the R478 brings you to the fishing village of **Liscannor**, birthplace of John Mulholland (1841–1914), inventor of the first successful submarine. On the road between Liscannor and the Cliffs of Moher are great slabs of stone used as field fencing. They have worm-like encrustations of marine life from the time when this region was well below sea level. These slabs, known as Liscannor slate, are still widely used as flooring in traditional cottages and pubs.

Cliffs of Moher

All roads around here lead to the ★★★ **Cliffs of Moher**, or so it seems from the innumerable signposts. Park at the **Visitor Centre** (March to November daily 9am–6pm), which offers another introduction to the flora and fauna of the area. Do not be put off by the crowds and the buskers at the bottom of the hill – the razzmatazz is easy to escape by simply walking up to the cliffs themselves. The best view is from **O'Brien's Tower**, which was built in 1853 by a local eccentric. On a clear day you can see all the way south to Loop Head, with the three Aran Islands out to sea, and the blue-tinged coast of Connemara visible in the north on the far side of Galway Bay.

The great, dark shale and sandstone cliffs are magnificent, rising 200m (650ft) sheer above the Atlantic and stretching for about 8km (5 miles). At their base the Atlantic waves throw white spume on to jagged stacks. Over the years the pounding has eroded the cliffs creating caves and bays which fill with dramatic waves, sending mist and spray high up the rock face. In summer you can spot comical-looking puffins nesting on the ledges, while numerous other seabirds wheel around in the up-currents.

Tiny Doolin

★ **Doolin** (also called Roadford on some maps) is a tiny village consisting of numerous B&Bs and hostels, several restaurants and three pubs. The pubs are renowned for traditional music. Some young musicians spend the whole summer camping here, learning from their elders. The bar food is excellent too – on a cold day warm up with a bowl of Irish stew in Gus O'Connor's.

There is a 45-minute open-boat ferry from Doolin pier to **Inishere**, the smallest of the **Aran Islands**, which makes an interesting day trip in calm weather (mid-March to October, tel. 065/74455 for details). Bigger, more comfortable boats leave for the islands from Rossaveale and Galway city (*see Route 3 and Practical Information, p75*).

Doolin Ferry to Inishere

Beyond Doolin the deeply fissured limestone plateau of the ★★★ **Burren** dominates. The limestone is revealed in great irregular pavements known as clints, with deep cracks between them, called grykes. Their geological name is Karst, from an area in Yugoslavia with similar terrain. Turloughs, seasonal lakes which disappear underground in dry weather, appear at times on the surface. As far as the eye can see the landscape is grey, which comes as a shock after the predominant green of the rest of Ireland. So barren did it look to Cromwell's troops in the 17th century that they declared that here was neither wood to hang a man, water to drown him nor earth to bury him.

As if to make the landscape even stranger, huge boulders were deposited on top of the limestone at the end of the Ice Age. It is sometimes hard to tell which boulder is an ice-age erratic, and which is a megalithic tomb.

Burren boulders

23

The wild flowers – Alpine, Arctic and Mediterranean – which so excite botanists are at their best in May. This is a small-scale spectacle, which you will not see without taking a walk. Look right down into the cracks between the limestone, and you will be amazed at what is growing there. Honeysuckle in particular thrives, but there are also gentians, bloody cranes bill and white anemones.

The best Burren drive goes inland through **Lisdoonvarna**, an odd little spa town with hot water springs, where Ireland's bachelor farmers congregate in September for the light-hearted **Matchmaking Festival** at which they attempt, usually half-heartedly, to find a wife.

Continue down the switchback road known as ★ **Corkscrew Hill** (N67) to **Ballyvaughan**, a lively little seaside village, returning to Lisdoonvarna around **Black Head** on the R477. Beyond Black Head, the three **Aran Islands** are visible in the west. In some weathers they appear to be floating and drifting, due to tricks of light.

Ailwee Cave

It is worth stopping at Ballyvaughan to visit ★ **Ailwee Cave** (mid-March to November, daily 10am–5.30pm). The guided tour takes you through a tunnel stretching for 1km (¾ mile) which contains stalactites and stalagmites, and ends at a waterfall floodlit from below.

If you are interested in visiting prehistoric remains, then take a detour up the R480 which leads to **Gleninsheen** wedge-shaped megalithic tombs which date from 1500BC, ★ **Poulnabrone**, a Neolithic dolmen whose cap stone probably weighs about 10 tons, and **Caherconnell**, a massive stone fort with concentric stone walls.

Poulnabrone dolmen

From Ballyvaughan take the N67 to Kinvara, turning left on to the N18 at Kilcogan for Galway.

Colourful Galway City

Route 3

Galway City and the Aran Islands

A centre of Irish tradition

Galway is a lively, compact city with a stylish young population of around 60,000. It is the fastest growing city in Ireland. Good road and rail links with Dublin make it a popular weekend destination: not only is its bracing Atlantic air a tonic, it is also one of the most active centres for the arts in Ireland. About 20 percent of Galway's population are students, either at its Regional Technical College or at its University which is an important centre for Irish language and Celtic studies. There is a decidedly Bohemian feel to the centre of Galway, and this its not only due to the fact that such a small city has three resident theatre companies and innumerable visual artists. Galway is the only place in Ireland where the local people habitually wear imaginatively designed hand-made clothes that are sold in the better craft shops. They look great, and add enormously to the atmosphere.

The Salmon Weir Bridge

Galway was founded on the estuary of the River Corrib in the late 12th century by Norman traders who enclosed the city with a defensive wall. The dominance of the original 14 families led to Galway's nickname, 'the City of Tribes'. The names of those 'tribes' are still common today in Galway and the rest of Ireland: Athy, Blake, Bodkin, Browne, D'Arcy, Dean, Font, French, Kirwan, Joyce, Lynch, Morris, Martin and Skerret. Much of Galway's trade, until the 17th century, was with the West Indies, France and Spain. The Spanish connection and the city's medieval origins have created a distinctive architecture which favours heavy stone door lintels, carved stone coats of arms and narrow two and three-storey townhouses huddled together on cobbled streets and alleyways.

One of the less attractive results of Galway's rapid growth is traffic gridlock in July and August, and long hold-ups all year round. There are plans for pedestrianisation, but this could take years. The sights of Galway can be visited on foot in a couple of hours, but as Galway's historic centre coincides with its commercial centre you may well get distracted by the shops, bars and cafés, so allow a full morning or afternoon.

Eyre Square is the centre of Galway, and its largest open space. Its southern side is dominated by the Great Southern Hotel, the only vaguely formal venue in a largely informal city. To the west of the hotel is the railway station, and down an alley on its east is the Tourist Information Office. At the centre of the square is the **John F. Kennedy Memorial Park ❶**, which commemorates the US President who visited here in June, 1963. The limestone statue celebrates a Galway storyteller, Pádraig O Conaire. The **Browne Doorway**, with its 17th-century coat of arms, was rescued in 1905 from a crumbling town house. Look out for similar features as you walk around the city. The steel sculpture standing in a fountain recalls the brown sails of the Galway hookers, traditional sailing boats.

Leave Eyre Square by the northwest corner and turn down Williamsgate Street. This leads to the River Corrib, changing its name four times on the way, becoming William, Shop, High and Quay Street. Look out above the shop fronts for carved coats of arms and old stone lintels. **Lynch's Castle ❷** (now Allied Irish Bank) at the

Pádraig O Conaire in Eyre Square

The Browne Doorway

25

**ROUTE 3
GALWAY CITY**

0   200m
0   200 yds

To University

Newcastle Road
Presentation Road
St Vincents Avenue
Headford Road
St Francis Street
Eglinton St.
Eyre Street
Prospect Hill
Mill Street
Nuns Island Road
Abbeygate St.
Nora Barnacle House
William Street
Eyre Square
Forster Street
Great Southern Hotel
Bridge Street
Shop Street
High St.
Tourist Information Centre
O'Briens Bridge
Quay St.
Tíg Neáchtain
Galway Station
William Street
Dominick Street
Wolfe Tone Bridge
Merchants Road
Dock Road
Father Griffin Road
Claddagh Quay
Spanish Arch
Lough Atalia Road

26

corner of William and Abbeygate streets, is the finest surviving example of a fortified 16th-century town house. Details of its stone lintels recall those found in southern Spain. Continue down Shop Street and turn right up the pedestrian alley. The **Lynch Memorial Window ❸** bears a skull and crossbones and was erected in 1624 with the inscription 'This memorial to the stern and unbending justice of the chief magistrate of this City, James Lynch FitzStephen, elected mayor AD1493, who condemned and executed his own son, Walter, on this spot'.

Adjacent is the **Collegiate Church of St Nicholas ❹** (daily 8am to dusk). Founded by the Normans in 1320, this is one of the best preserved medieval churches in Ireland. It is said that Columbus prayed here before setting off on his voyage to America. On Saturday mornings a small street market is held in the alley beside the church, selling fresh local produce and some crafts.

Nora Barnacle House (mid-May to mid-September, Monday to Saturday 2am–5pm; off-season by appointment, tel: 091/564743), where the wife of James Joyce grew up, is close to St Nicholas, and displays a collection of photographs and memorabilia.

Follow High Street through to Quay Street and to ★ **Tíg Neáchtain** or Noctan's, one of Galway's most famous pubs. It does excellent bar food and is also the place to go to find out what's happening on the arts scene. Continue along this lively stretch of Quay Street down to the River Corrib. Those interested in modern design should not miss **Design Concourse Ireland** in Kirwan's Lane behind the Spanish Arch Hotel. This gallery and retail outlet is a showcase of the best in Irish crafts.

The **Spanish Arch** was part of a fort built in 1584 to protect the quays where the Spanish ships landed their cargoes. It is now marooned in a car park opposite Jury's Inn. Next door is the **Galway City Museum ❺** (mid-March to September, daily 10am–1pm and 2.15–5.15pm; October to mid-March, Tuesday to Thursday same hours), an old fashioned civic museum with items of local history.

Across the river is **The Claddagh ❻**. Until 1927 this was an area of thatched cottages where the fishermen lived. It was ruled by its own elected 'king', the last of whom died in 1934. Nowadays it is indistinguishable from any other area of municipal housing, but the name lives on in the **Claddagh ring**. The ring shows two clasped hands around a heart, and is often used as a wedding ring.

Cross the Corrib on the Wolfe Tone Bridge and turn right on to the footpath. The second bridge along is ★★★ **The Salmon Weir Bridge ❼**, which provides a natural spectacle from mid-April to early July, when shoals of salmon can be seen lying in the clear water, waiting to make their way up the Corrib to spawn. From the bridge, too, there is a view of the **Cathedral of Our Lady Assumed into Heaven and St Nicholas** ❽, built in 1965. Beyond the church is the Tudor-Gothic style quadrangle of the **University of Galway**, founded in 1845. The library has an important archive of Celtic materials.

Cathedral window

It is just a short (1.6km/1 mile) walk from Wolfe Tone Bridge to **Salthill**, a place of B&Bs and budget hotels, many facing the seaside promenade. The walk is popular among Galwegians, particularly on a Sunday afternoon.

The Aran Islands

The ★★★ **Aran Islands** lie across the mouth of Galway Bay, about 48km (30 miles) offshore. There is a choice of ferry (about an hour and a half) or light aircraft (six minutes), and numerous ticket deals, many of which include one night's B&B. These are Irish-speaking islands, where the old folklore and traditions persisted well into the mid-20th century. But better education, better transport, television and tourism have all played their part in diluting the essential difference of the islands. Do not expect to walk into a living folk park. Aran Islanders still speak Irish, but nowadays they wear sneakers and jeans and watch colour TV just like the rest of us. Nevertheless, a visit to the islands can be a memorable and enlightening experience. The boat trip offers exhilarating views (weather permitting) of Connemara, the Burren and the open sea. The best time to go is between April and October, but outside the high season. The islands receive over 100,000 visitors a year, many of them in July and August, and there is talk of introducing ticket-rationing.

The Arans have a slower pace

The islands are officially part of County Galway, and culturally they have much in common with the Irish-speaking coast of Connemara, but geologically they belong to the Burren, sharing the distinctive landscape of limestone

Aran Islands beach

pavements. The islands also contain a wealth of pre-Christian and early Christian remains.

Life out in the wild Atlantic was hard. The limestone landscape meant there was hardly any soil on the islands: arable plots had to be created by carrying seaweed and sand from the shore, and enclosing the space with stone walls to stop it blowing away. Fields on the islands are tiny, supporting perhaps one cow or two sheep. Islanders fished from currachs – light-framed, tarred canvas boats that could take the greatest Atlantic waves when rowed by skilful hands. They fashioned their own footwear, called pampooties, a heel-less leather shoe suitable for jumping form rock to rock, and naturally waterproofed sweaters or 'ganseys'. The design on the ganseys was often the only way of identifying a body lost at sea.

Aran heritage

In the late 19th century the islands were discovered as a living repository of folklore and language by members of the Gaelic Revival. J.M. Synge (1871–1909) lived in a simple cottage on Inishere while learning Irish, and used the stories told around the fire in his West of Ireland plays. In 1934 Robert Flaherty made the classic documentary *Man of Aran*, which highlights the bravery and skill of the men who went to sea in currachs.

Inishmore is the largest island, about 13km (8 miles) long by 3km (2 miles) wide, with 900 inhabitants. It is also the most highly developed for tourism. Between May and October minibuses and ponies and traps meet the ferries, and bicycles can be hired at the pier. The **Aran Heritage Centre** (April to October, daily 10am–7pm) explains the history and culture of the islands. The best known sight

Dun Aengus

is ★★ **Dun Aengus**, one of the great Iron Age stone forts dating from about 550BC, which was built on the brink of a sheer cliff. It consists of three concentric rows of defences around a cliff edge with a sheer drop of 60m (200ft) to the sea. There are numerous B&Bs, and a choice of pub restaurants, some offering live entertainment.

Inishmaan, the middle island in size and position, with a population of 300, is the least developed for tourism, still relying largely on farming and fishing. To explore its cliff walks and secluded coves and its early Christian remains

Inishere

you must go on foot. ★★ **Inishere** is the smallest and flattest of the islands, the most Burren-like in vegetation, and the only one with a stretch of sandy beach, very popular with the many Irish schoolchildren sent here in August to study the language. Those fields that are not under cultivation turn into spectacular wild flower meadows in the summer. The island can be explored by a network of footpaths, many enclosed by tall stone walls. Don't miss the 'back of the island', an uninhabited area whose rocks are pounded by the mighty Atlantic ocean.

Route 4

South Galway

Galway – Clarinbridge – Kinvara – Thoor Ballylee – Coole Park (61km/38 miles)

Short in distance, but rich in interesting places to visit, this leisurely day trip travels south from Galway through oyster country to visit Kinvara, a small and characterful fishing village on the edge of Galway Bay dominated by the beautifully located Dunguaire Castle. South of Kinvara and inland is the atmospheric tower house that Yeats restored in the 1920s, Thoor Ballylee. Nearby Kiltartan Cross and Coole Park are also closely associated with the poet Yeats and with his benefactor Lady Gregory.

Clarinbridge oysters

Leave Galway on the N6, joining the N18 Gort–Ennis road at Oranmore. **Clarinbridge**, 9km (5½ miles) south of Oranmore, is the venue in early September for the first of Galway's two oyster festivals; the other is held in the city centre at the end of the month. Festivities centre around **Paddy Burke's pub**, a lively and characterful spot. However, many people prefer the quieter rural pleasures of a nearby waterside pub, ★★ **Moran's Oyster Cottage**. The turn-off to Moran's is indicated by a large sign on the right just beyond Clarinbridge in **Kilcolgan**. The tiny thatched cottage, which is beside a weir, has been famous for its oysters since 1760. The Morans have retained the layout of the original family cottage, and a visit to the front

Paddy Burke's Pub

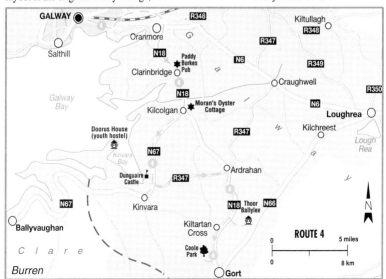

ROUTE 4

Kinvara

Dunguaire Castle

Thoor Ballylee

part of the house/bar with its wooden settles and benches shows how rooms were organised in small homes like this in the old days. At the back is a large cheerful restaurant, but you can also take an outside seat overlooking the weir. A pint of stout and a dozen oysters outside Moran's is one of the quintessential West of Ireland experiences that make people return again and again.

★★ **Kinvara**, 9.5km (6 miles) southwest of Kilcolgan, is a charming fishing village at the head of Galway Bay. You will pass **Dunguaire Castle** (mid-April to mid-June, Tuesday to Sunday 9.30am–6.30pm; mid-June to August, daily 9.30am–6.30pm; September, daily 10am–5pm; tel: 061/360788 to book for banquets) before entering the village. An impressive four-storey tower house, it stands by the shore at the head of **Kinvara Bay** which is in turn part of Galway Bay. At night it is used for medieval banquets.

Kinvara, with its grassy quays, friendly pubs, unusual craft shops and surprisingly cosmopolitan population of about 450 souls, is increasingly popular with visitors, who enjoy its old fashioned pubs and more up-to-the-minute restaurants. The elegant new **Merriman Inn** in the village centre is the largest thatched building in Ireland, and proof at last that not all modern Irish hotels are architectural disasters. The highlight of the Kinvara year is the annual **Cruinniú na mBád** in mid-August, literally 'the gathering of the boats'. This is a festive regatta in which traditional sailing craft – the brown-sailed Galway hookers – which were once used to carry turf across the bay, race against each other in a grand spectacle.

If the weather is good there is a pleasant drive for 22km (13½ miles) along the N67 to Ballyvaughan (*see Route 2, page 23*) which offers views of both the Burren and Galway Bay. Walkers might like to explore the two small peninsulas west of Kinvara that jut out into Galway Bay, peaceful places with small stony beaches, that overlook the grey rocks of the Burren. **Doorus House**, signposted these days as a youth hostel, was home to the affable Count Florimond de Basterot at the end of the 19th century. His family fled to Ireland at the time of the French revolution, but he kept up literary links with France, and entertained Guy de Maupassant here, along with Irish guests including his neighbours Lady Gregory and W.B. Yeats. It was during an idle afternoon at Doorus House that the idea of a National Theatre for Ireland was first mooted.

The easiest way back to the N18 from Kinvara is the R347 **Ardrahan** road. Turn right at the N18 in the Gort direction to visit ★ **Thoor Ballylee** (Easter to September, daily 10am–6pm), a 16th-century tower house beautifully situated in a wooded area near a stream, which was the summer home of W.B. Yeats from 1917 to 1928.

The property was discovered for the poet by his benefactor Lady Gregory (1852–1932), herself a playwright and collector of folklore and founder member of Ireland's National Theatre, the Abbey. Yeats bought it in 1916 for £35, but the increasing pressures of public duties after winning the Nobel Prize and being appointed to the Irish Senate left him little time to enjoy his tower. He last visited it in 1928, and after the death of Lady Gregory in 1932 the tower settled into a decline which he had anticipated in the poem *To be Carved on a Stone at Thoor Ballylee*:

'I the poet William Yeats
With old millboards and sea-green slates
And smithy work from the Gort forge
Restored this tower for my wife George.
And may these characters remain
When all is ruin once again.'

Nowadays the tower is carefully restored with much of Yeats' original furniture. The audio-visual presentation gives a witty and intelligent introduction to the poet's work and life.

Return to the N18 and head south. On the way to Coole Park you will pass **Kiltartan Cross**, whose inhabitants taught Lady Gregory so much about Irish folklore, and provided her with the model for native speech patterns which she used in her plays. Her house at **Coole Park** was demolished in 1947, but its grounds are now a national park with a deer enclosure, forest walks and a lake whose petrified trees stick out of the water. In the walled garden is a great copper beech tree on which Lady Gregory's guests carved their initials. Beside Yeats, George Bernard Shaw, J.M. Synge, John Masefield, Augustus John and Sean O'Casey all made their mark here.

Coole Park: autograph details

The copper beech is in the centre

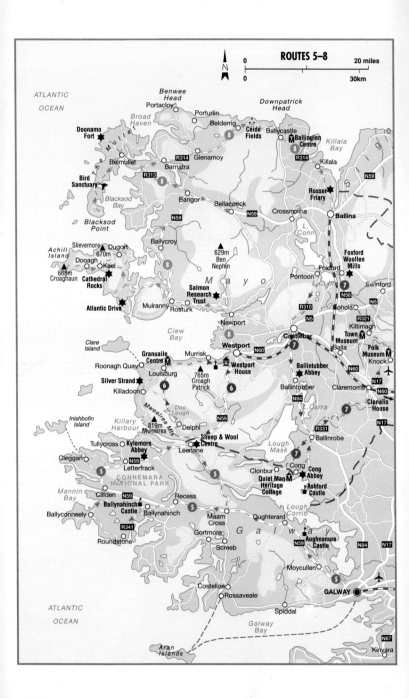

Route 5

Into Connemara

Moycullen – Oughterard – Ballynahinch – Roundstone
– Clifden – Inishbofin – Letterfrack – Leenane
(198km/123 miles) *See map opposite*

This route brings you into the heartland of the wild beauty
of the rugged western part of County Galway known as
Connemara. Lonely roads pass through silent boglands
past glacial lakes that reflect the blue of the sky. Heavy
rainfall and strong Atlantic winds lead to an almost total
absence of trees; the exceptions are modern conifer plantations that bring an attractive touch of green to the pre-
dominantly brown landscape. The Maamturks and the
Twelve Bens tower over vast stretches of moorland where
native Connemara ponies graze in the wild. The rocky
coastline contains numerous small bays and isolated sandy
beaches. This is a place to leave the car and walk to savour
in full the unpolluted Atlantic air, the unusual and surprisingly beautiful bogland flora and the ever-changing
views which vary dramatically according to the light of
the rapidly changing weather.

Twelve Bens moorland

Moycullen marble

33

The N59 out of Galway passes through **Moycullen**, with
its factory producing the distinctive green and black Connemara marble (open daily in summer). Skilled craftsmen
can be seen at work, and there is a variety of marble items
as well as jewellery and gifts for sale. There are glimpses
of Lough Corrib, Galway's watery interior, and the smaller
Ross Lake on the right of the road. A signpost about 3km
(2 miles) before Oughterard, near the golf club, directs the
visitor to **Aughnanure Castle** (mid-June to September
9.30am– 6.30pm). Built by an O'Flaherty in the 16th century on the shores of Lough Corrib, it is a picturesque
and well preserved example of a tower house with two fortified enclosures, a watch tower and a great hall.

Aughnanure Castle

Oughterard is a renowned game angling centre. To
reach ★ **Lough Corrib** take the lane beside the Health
Centre on the Galway side of the village. This is the place
to rent boats for a Corrib cruise. There are boats to **Cong**
on the Mayo shore or to **Inchagoill Island**, an uninhabited island with a couple of romantic ruins. The prettiest
part of Oughterard is the west side of town near **Sweeney's
Oughterard Hotel**, a quiet, old fashioned angler's hotel
beside a pleasantly wooded stretch of the **Owenriff River**.

Sweeney's Oughterard Hotel

This is the last wooded glade you will see for some time.
Connemara does not actually have fixed, statutory bor-
ders, but you will know it when you see it as you travel

A local maker of bodhrans (goatskin tambourines played with a small stick)

along the N59 to Maam Cross. Suddenly the landscape turns bare and deserted, yet remains strangely beautiful as the dramatic West of Ireland light plays on it contours, rendering it stark and forbidding in shade, the next minute bathing it in warm sunlight.

Apparently in the middle of nowhere, the crossroads of **Maam Cross** has always been a convenient central meeting and marketing place for sheep farmers from all four corners of Connemara. Nowadays it also has a handy petrol station and the inevitable craft shop.

The original settlements of Connemara were all near the coast; the interior, then as now, was virtually uninhabited. An ancient 65-km (40 mile) packhorse trail ran across the bog from Oughterard to the Martin estate at Ballynahinch (*see below*). In 1818 Thomas Martin secured government funding for a road across the bog to replace the pack horse trail. It was completed in 1835, carried out largely as relief work created to relieve poverty and distress rather than because anyone, other than the Martins, actually wanted it. The same engineer responsible for this and the rest of the Connemara road network, Scotsman Alexander Nimmo, also designed the harbours at Cleggan, Clifden, Roundstone and Rossaveale, thus transforming the lives of the local fishermen.

Continue through **Recess** and about 19km (12 miles) beyond Maam Cross turn left off N59 onto the R341. ★★ **Ballynahinch Castle**, now a hotel, stands in wooded grounds beside a tranquil lake. Even if your budget does not allow you to stay here, drop by for coffee or bar food to get a feeling of how the rich once lived in Connemara.

Ballynahinch Castle

The Martins, a wealthy merchant family, acquired the house and lakelands after its confiscation by Cromwell. The present structure was built around 1720 and enlarged in 1813. The most famous Martin, Richard Martin

(1754–1834), acquired contradictory nicknames – 'Humanity Dick' – for his kindness to animals and as founder of the Royal Society for the Prevention of Cruelty to Animals (RSPCA), and 'Hairtrigger Dick' for his quick recourse to duelling to settle disputes. Likewise he lived a dual existence – as a fashionable gentleman in London society in the early 18th century, and as a feudal landlord here at home. When his friend the Prince Regent boasted of the great drive at Windsor, Dick Martin retorted, quite accurately, that his drive was 40 miles long. Overspending by the family and the advent of the Famine finally bankrupted the estate. In 1925 the cricketer Prince Ranjit Sinjhi became the owner of the remaining demesne which later passed to a Dublin businessman.

From here the choice of route depends on the weather. If it is overcast, rainy or misty (or a combination of all three) return to the N59 and head directly for Clifden (about 12km/8 miles). If the sun is shining, even intermittently, take the longer coast route, travelling to Clifden on the R341 via Roundstone (about 37km/23 miles).

★ **Roundstone**, with its lovely bay, is a lively place with fine sandy beaches at Dog's Bay. It is popular with both writers and artists. The novelist Kate O'Brien (1897–1974) spent her summers here towards the end of her life, while Tim Robinson, artist, author and inspired cartographer who has contributed so much in recent years to our understanding of Connemara and the Aran Islands, lives and works here year round. Also on this road, 5km (3 miles) south of Clifden, is a **memorial** marking the 1919 landing of the first people to fly non-stop across the Atlantic, Alcock and Brown.

Roundstone bay and beach

The sand from the dunes of Ballyconneely and its golf course frequently covers the R341 to ★ **Clifden**, Connemara's main centre. With only about 1,200 residents, Clifden would barely qualify as a town in most places, but out here it is something of a metropolis, referred to without irony as 'the capital of Connemara'. Its location on a tall cliff overlooking Clifden Bay, backed by the Twelve Ben mountains, is outstanding, but in fact it looks better from a distance than it feels when you are in it. The best way to orient yourself in Clifden is to walk or drive the first mile or so of the Sky Road, a scenic route that travels above the town giving panoramic views of the bay.

Clifden

The town is not an old one. It was founded by an improving landlord, John D'Arcy, in the 1820s. It offers a good choice of restaurants, pub entertainment and craft shops, but can get very overcrowded and noisy at night in July and August. Clifden is the headquarters of the **Connemara Pony Society**, formed in 1923 to ensure standards of breeding in this hardy mountain pony valued for its

Letterfrack woodworker

Connemara farmer

Crafts at Kylemore

docile temperament and intelligence. The annual **Connemara Pony Show** adds to August's chaos on the third Thursday in the month.

Cleggan, 9km (5½ miles) northwest of Clifden, is the departure point for the island of ★★★ **Inishbofin** 11km (7 miles) offshore. Boffin, as it is known, is an English-speaking island with a seasonal population of about 200 (they come ashore for the winter). Day trip tickets are available from April to September, but there is also plenty of overnight accommodation. Inishbofin is a gentle sort of place after Connemara, with basking seals in its sheltered coves, heathery moorland and the calm waters of **Lough Boffin**, circled by bulrushes and wild iris. Because the islanders do not use modern agricultural methods, Boffin is something of a nature reserve, and one of the few places where the corn crake can still be heard.

The N59 continues to **Letterfrack** and the ★ **Connemara National Park**. There is a **Visitor Centre** (May and September daily 10am–5.30pm; June, July and August daily 10am–6.30pm) covering the area's history and ecology and giving details of local walks.

Most visitors are stopped in their tracks by the first view of ★★ **Kylemore Abbey** (April to September, daily 9.30am–6.30pm), a huge grey crenellated building backed by a wooded hill behind a lake whose placid waters provide a perfect reflection on calm days. Currently a boarding school run by Benedictine nuns, it was built by the MP for Galway, Mitchell Henry, for his ailing wife in 1864. The hall, Gothic chapel and three reception rooms are open to visitors. There is also a craft shop and restaurant.

★ **Killary Harbour** is a long narrow inlet reminiscent of a Norwegian fjord. The inlet runs for 16km (10 miles) with the steep face of Mweelrea (819m/2,685ft) forming its north side. The dots that run in lines on its surface are floating fish farms. While they may mar the pristine beauty of Ireland's only fjord, they also provide much needed jobs for local people. At the head of the harbour is the village of **Leenane**, where angling and mountain climbing are major attractions. It was location for the 1990 film *The Field*, starring Richard Harris, a painfully accurate portrait of rural Ireland's obsession with land ownership.

Leenane's ★ **Sheep and Wool Centre** (April to October 9.30am–7pm), situated on the Clifden–Westport road, covers the traditional industry of the area, sheep rearing and wool production. Some twenty breeds of sheep graze around the house, and all aspects of wool production are entertainingly explained.

From Leenane take the R345 southwards to Maam Cross to return to Galway, or continue north for Westport (*see Route 6*).

Route 6

Fireman Sam at the Clew Bay Heritage Centre

The Doo Lough Valley to Clew Bay

Leenane – Doo Lough – Clare Island – Louisburgh – Murrisk – Croagh Patrick – Westport (64km/40 miles)
See map, page 32

37

This route takes us north from Connemara into County Mayo, a large, sparsely populated area of the western seaboard. The route via Louisburgh skirts the slopes of Mweelrea Mountain as it approaches the conical shape of Croagh Patrick, which dominates the skyline for miles around. The Reek, as it is known locally, still attracts thousands of pilgrims every year who climb its 765-m (2,510ft) in honour of Saint Patrick who is traditionally said to have wrestled with the devil on its summit. Croagh Patrick overlooks island-studded Clew Bay, where Clare Island was once the fortress home of the west of Ireland's great sea pirate, Grace O'Malley or Granuaile, a contemporary of England's Queen Elizabeth I. Westport is a lively market town whose wide streets and tree-lined mall were laid out by the local landowner, the Earl of Altamont, in the 18th century. Westport House, home of the present day Earl, is open to the public.

Croagh Patrick

Leave **Leenane** on the N59 travelling north. Three kilometres (2 miles) outside Leenane there is a left-hand turn which is the longer and more scenic route to Westport (about 48km/30 miles). If the weather does not favour leisurely sightseeing, keep straight on the N59 which leads to Westport in about half the distance. On both roads, look out for the bulk of Croagh Patrick whose conical summit may well be shrouded in mist, whatever the weather. There is a gloomy local saying in this windswept coastal

Aasleagh Falls

area whose high mountains make it even more prone than other parts of the west to sudden rain showers: if you can't see the tip of the Reek it is raining; if you can see it, it is about to rain.

The R335 follows the north shore of Killary harbour for about 8km (5 miles) before turning due north. Shortly after turning off the main road you drive by the River Errif. You can park at the bridge, and from here you will hear the sound of the **Aasleagh Falls** gently cascading over a series of naturally formed steps. A little stile leads right to the water's edge, a fine place to savour the splendour of the green mountains and the emptiness of the landscape.

As the road continues the **Sheefry Hills** lie to the east of it, with the **Mweelrea Mountains** in the west. This is one of the most beautiful of many impressive scenic drives in the West of Ireland. An early devotee of this part of the world was the local landlord, the Marquess of Sligo, a friend of Lord Byron, who named the area **Delphi** on his return from the Grand Tour, as he reckoned its beauty could match anything he had seen in Greece. **Delphi Lodge**, the large lakeside house visible from the road, offers accommodation to game anglers and other lovers of solitude.

Delphi's original name was Fionnloch or 'white lake', to distinguish it from the next landmark on this route, ★★★**Doo Lough**, or 'dark lake'. When the sun shines there are wonderful views over the lake and river and beyond the Mweelrea, enhanced by a constantly changing light which frequently refracts into rainbows. However, on a dark day with lashing rain the largely uninhabited moorland can also seem eerie and inhospitable.

A simple roadside cross near Doo Lough recalls a tragic event from the years of the Great Famine. In 1849, when people all over Mayo were dying of starvation, a rumour started in Louisburgh that there was plentiful food avail-

Doo Lough

able at Delphi where a group of local dignitaries had gathered for a meeting. About five hundred desperate men, women and children set out to walk from Louisburgh to Delphi, a journey of about 32km (20 miles) before the modern road was built. When they arrived they were told there was nothing for them, so they turned around to walk home again. The weather was atrocious, and when they reached the place near Doo Lough where they had crossed the river on their outward trek, it was so swollen as to be almost impassable. Weakened by hunger and by their long walk, over half, possibly two-thirds of the starving people were swept away by floods. This tragic event is still remembered hereabouts.

There is an optional detour off the main road to Louisburgh at a signpost on the left for **Killadoon**. The road runs through attractive, soft green countryside, where the hills are covered in purple heather in late summer. It leads to a mile-long beach called the **Silver Strand** where Atlantic rollers crash on to the shore.

High summer on Clare Island

39

★★ **Clare Island** is visible from the Silver Strand, and the ferry can be reached by turning left before entering Louisburgh at signs for **Roonagh Quay**. The ferry takes about 25 minutes (at least two crossings daily, weather permitting). The island is tiny – 5.5km by 2.5km (½ by 1½ miles) – and has a population of 140. Popular with divers, sea anglers, and walkers, it rises to a height of about 500m (1,650ft) and has dramatic western cliffs. Dolphins, seals and otters as well as interesting sea birds can be observed. The square tower on a rocky headland at the harbour is one of many castles in this area associated with Grace O'Malley, or Granuaile as she is called in Irish. This remarkable 16th-century sea-queen lived by piracy and plunder. So powerful was she that when she visited the court of Queen Elizabeth I she was received with full honours. History tells us that these two formidable women conversed in Latin, Granuaile having never mastered the English language. She died in her seventies in 1603, and is buried in the tiny abbey, now ruined, on Clare Island.

Clare Island ferry

★ **Louisburgh** (pronounced Lewis-burg), a pleasant if somewhat run-down little town, is also associated with Granuaile, and at the **Granuaile Centre** (June to August, Monday to Saturday 10am–6pm, Sunday 11am–5pm) can learn more about the pirate queen, and the area in general. Louisburgh was named after Louisburgh, Nova Scotia, which the uncle of the first Marquess of Sligo helped to capture in 1758. The Centre also has details of the annual **Great Famine Walk** which commemorates the tragedy at Doo Lough.

The road from Louisburgh to Westport runs through **Murrisk**, which is the traditional starting point for the as-

Grace O'Malley's last resting place

At the base of Croagh Patrick

cent of ★★★ **Croagh Patrick**. The wide path can be seen winding gently up the hill. It is not a difficult climb, as long as you are reasonably fit, the worst part being a seemingly endless stretch of loose scree leading to the summit. Locals use a sturdy, shoulder-high walking stick called an ash plant to get a grip. On the last Sunday in July these are sold in the car park, and about 25,000 people, mostly simple country folk, will climb the Reek as a penance, many of them barefoot. The tiny white oratory on the summit was built in 1905, the materials carried up by pilgrims. The round trip takes about three hours. Even if you only make it halfway, the views of Clew Bay are spectacular.

Overlooking the waters of Clew Bay, the **Westport Quays** begin about 8km (5 miles) beyond Murrisk. Once an almost derelict area, the old warehouses have recently been converted into holiday apartments. There is a lively pub and restaurant scene around the quays, and amenities for deep sea angling and sailing. Art and antique galleries and craft shops are also proliferating here. The **Clew Bay Heritage Centre** is a focal point for local art and culture.

Westport House interior

Keep straight on for ★ **Westport House** (grounds and house, June daily 2–6pm, July to August daily 10.30am–6pm; house only, May and September daily 2–6pm), seat of the Earl of Altamont, the present day heir of the Marquess of Sligo. This was designed and built by Richard Cassels in 1730. The dungeons belonged to an earlier castle, believed to have been the home of the ubiquitous Grace O'Malley. Contents include early Irish silver, early Waterford crystal, late Georgian and early Victorian furniture and pictures. Much of the estate is given over to attractions for children, including a zoo, miniature railway, model railway, slides, dungeons and camping park. Parents be warned, this can be an expensive outing!

Westport: shop and souvenirs

★★ **Westport** itself, with a population of about 4,000 and growing, lies slightly inland. It was designed by James Wyatt in the Georgian style to complement Westport House, and features a central octagon and a mall of lime trees through which the Carrowbeg river runs, the two connected by wide, hilly streets. There is an old-fashioned farmer's market in the Octagon on Thursday mornings (also Friday and Saturday in summer) which sells weatherproof work-gear alongside fresh local produce. Many of Westport's shops are similarly old-fashioned, particularly in their window displays. Westport has only recently woken up to the 20th century. An assortment of multi-national high-tech factories provides much-needed jobs for its young people, while its short summer season is enlivened by a cosmopolitan crowd of visitors. Not only is it the most attractively designed town in County Mayo; nowadays it is also the liveliest.

Route 7

Ballintuber Abbey

Inland County Mayo and Lough Corrib

Castlebar – Ballintubber – Ballinrobe – Cong – Claremorris – Knock– Kiltimagh – Foxford – Pontoon
(138km/86 miles) *See map, page 32*

This route explores inland County Mayo and offers several options which will appeal in rainy weather. From
Castlebar, administrative capital of Co. Mayo, we travel
south along the shores of Lough Mask to Cong on Lough
Corrib. There is an optional excursion to Clonalis House,
ancestral home of the O'Connor clan. Knock is an important centre of pilgrimage for Catholics, while the village of Kiltimagh pays homage to the rural past. Foxford
offers tours of a fully restored woollen mill, while pretty
Pontoon is a renowned angling centre.

Castlebar is the administrative capital of Co. Mayo and
has a population of 6,000. The landlord hereabouts is Lord
Lucan, and the leaseholders of Castlebar are particularly
interested in a resolution of the mystery of the missing
British peer, who disappeared following the murder of his
nanny in 1974, but to whom they still have to pay rent.

Castlebar

Take the N84 southwards to Ballintubber. **Ballintubber Abbey** was built on the site of a church associated with
St Patrick. It is the starting point of a 35-km (22 mile) long
pilgrim's path to Croagh Patrick, which is still walked
today. Founded in 1216 by the king of Connacht, Cathal
O'Connor, for the Augustinians, the abbey survived suppression by Henry VIII and further destruction by Oliver
Cromwell in 1653. Although roofless for 250 years, it continued as a place of regular worship. It has been somewhat
over-restored of late.

Continue southwards on the N84, past the shores of Lough Carra and Lough Mask – wide expanses of water, popular with game anglers. South of Ballinrobe, between Lough Mask and Lough Corrib, is the pretty, old world village of **Cong**. It takes its name from the narrow neck of land, *conga* in Irish on which is situated. John Ford's celebrated 1952 film *The Quiet Man*, starring John Wayne and Maureen O'Hara, was shot here. The **Quiet Man Heritage Cottage** (March to November, daily 10am–6pm) will appeal to both movie buffs and people nostalgic for the recent past. **Cong Abbey** was founded for the Augustinians by Rory O'Connor, last High King of Ireland, who died in 1198. Some beautiful window and door carvings can still be seen.

South of the abbey, a pedestrian entrance leads you over a bridge to the castellated ★ **Ashford Castle**, now an American-run luxury hotel. Built in 1870 and incorporating a much earlier tower house, it was one of the country houses of the Guinness family. It retains much of its original and unusual character, and is beautifully situated on the shores of **Lough Corrib**. The main rooms have handsome fireplaces with cowl-type chimney breasts and wood-panelled walls above which hang large oil paintings in gilt frames. Great windows open southwards to the formal garden and a view of Lough Corrib. Even if only visited for morning coffee or afternoon tea, the relaxing effect of gracious comfort should be a tonic.

Asford Castle: interior and fireplace detail

Return to Ballinrobe and take the R331 east, to the busy market town of **Claremorris**. Here there is an optional detour 37km (23 miles) east via Ballyhaunis to Castlerea where you can visit ★ **Clonalis House** (June to mid-September, Tuesday to Sunday 11am to 5pm; guided tour only; *see map, page 56*). This is the ancestral seat of the head of the O'Connor clan, who have owned this land for over 1,500 years. The present Italianate house, which stands above the River Suck, dates only from 1878. It is sumptuously furnished, with portraits of famous O'Connors, an interesting collection of porcelain, 18th and 19th-century Irish furniture and a small museum containing letters and archives. Look out for the harp that belonged to Turlough O'Carolan, the blind harpist and composer who was a frequent visitor to the house.

The main route continues north on the N17 across flat, unappealing countryside to **Knock**. An apparition of the Virgin Mary was seen in 1879 at the gable of a church in the village. It lasted for two hours and was witnessed by 15 people of varying ages. Knock today is an important Marian shrine. Cures have been claimed by sick and disabled pilgrims. Knock is no longer a village but an expanding town which can accommodate 12,000 visitors. An ornate

The Marian shrine at Knock

basilica, built in 1976, dwarfs the old church. Rows of shops are filled with religious souvenirs. Between May and October the devotional atmosphere can be quite moving, as large groups of pilgrims encircle the buildings while reciting the Rosary aloud. An energetic cleric, the late Monsignor James Horan is credited with much of the achievement – building the basilica, lobbying for an international airport nearby and gaining the Papal imprimatur with the visit of Pope John Paul II in 1979. Some visitors are put off by the excesses of Knock – holy water gushes of taps in the car park, most souvenirs are tawdry, and the architecture is painfully ostentatious – but it bears witness to a form of Catholicism which persists even today in other, chiefly agricultural communities throughout Europe, and indeed the world.

Among the souvenirs

Even those with little religious inclination should find the **Folk Museum** (May to October 10am–6pm, July to August 10am–7pm) interesting. Although it also contains documentation concerning the apparition, it deals extensively with rural life through the 19th century. Exhibits include kitchenware, utensils, fireplace irons, tools, modes of transport, costumes and early labour-saving devices.

43

Leave Knock on the R323 heading northwest for the village of ★ **Kiltimagh**, pronounced 'Kulchie-mock'. It is the origin of the modern Irish word, 'culchie', a term used, usually in a derogatory way, to indicate someone of obvious rural origins. It arose because so many people from this part of Mayo emigrated to Dublin and elsewhere in search of work in the past 150 years. The Kiltimagh railway station, from which so many emigrants left, has been restored, and houses the **Town Museum and Art Exhibitions Centre** (June to September, daily 2–6pm) with a sculpture park in the surrounding grounds. The forge and the old schoolhouse have also been converted into heritage centres. Kiltimagh today is a lively, brightly painted village, bursting with civic pride, a far cry from the old 'culchie' image.

Continue north on the R321 to Bohola, turning left to reach the N58 and Foxford. **Foxford Woollen Mills** (Monday to Saturday 10am–6pm, Sunday noon–6pm) is advertised far and wide in this part of the world. Shopping is one option, but there is also an interesting guided tour of the woollen mill which was founded by the Sisters of Charity in the 1850s to provide famine relief employment.

At the Foxford Woollen Mills

A drive on the R318 around the shores of Lough Cullin leads to the charming lakeside village of **Pontoon**, whose bridge offers views of both Lough Cullin in the south and Lough Conn in the north. It is renowned for game fishing and coarse fishing. **Pontoon Bridge Hotel** teaches casting and fly-fishing. The R310 returns to Castlebar.

Newport

Route 8

Achill Island and the North Mayo Coast

**Newport– Mulranny – Achill Island – Erris – Belmullet
– Céide Fields – Ballycastle – Downpatrick Head –
Killala – Ballina (190km/120 miles)** *See map, page 32*

Starting from the elegant little town of Newport, this route
takes in the most westerly peninsula of County Mayo
which juts out into the Atlantic ocean. Achill, Ireland's
largest island, is connected by a causeway to the mainland,
and is a popular destination offering fuchsia-lined lanes
in summer months. Belmullet to the north is a harsher,
more exposed place, a fishing community which attracts
fewer visitors. The route then crosses an area of sparsely
inhabited bog to the cliffs of Belderrig and the Céide
Fields, which displays Europe's greatest treasury of farming archaeology, ending in the busy cross-road town, Ballina. These are the lesser known parts of the West where,
even in the peak tourist season, roads remain uncrowded.

Newport House

Newport is situated on the Beltra River 12km (7miles)
north of Westport on the N59. The viaduct over the estuary, with seven arches of dressed stone, was built in 1892
to carry the train from Westport to Achill. **Newport House**
situated by the quay is a handsome, creeper-clad Georgian
country house hotel, owned by descendants of the Earls
of Tyrconnell (Ulster) who were transplanted to Mayo
by Oliver Cromwell. It is an architectural gem, with fine
plasterwork and a striking staircase with lantern and dome.
There is private salmon fishing in the grounds.

Newport's old-style shop fronts painted in prime colours
line each side of the rising main street, that drops away

through a rather dangerous narrow corner before heading westward for the fuchsia and rhododendrons of Mulranny. A few miles outside Newport, a sign on the N59 points to Furnace and the ★ **Salmon Research Trust** (June to September daily 10am–5.30pm) which concerns itself with the life-history of salmon and sea trout and the management of stocks. There are freshwater and marine aquaria, plus audio-visual presentations.

Salmon Research Trust

There are excellent sea views between Rosturk and **Mulranny**. The latter was until quite recently a popular resort created by the early railway. A grand hotel, which once featured a seawater swimming pool, overlooks the bay, standing vacant. John Lennon and Yoko Ono stayed here in the late sixties soon after they met, in a successful attempt to escape the attentions of Lennon's fans. Mulranny beach holds an European Union Blue Flag award.

★★★ **Achill Island** is connected to the mainland by a causeway with a narrow lifting bridge. It reaches the island though the village of Achill Sound. Achill measures 24km by 19km (15 by 12 miles) and has a population of about 1,000. It has three rounded mountain peaks, one or other of which seems to be always in view. Your impression of Achill is likely to depend very much on the weather. When the sun shines its cliffs and its deserted golden beaches, its turquoise sea, and its narrow, fuchsia-lined lanes, can make it seem a magical place. In windy, rainy weather you are more likely to notice the unfortunate developments of suburban-type modern bungalows for local residents, the proliferation of clusters of concrete houses, in which the local planning authority decrees that tourists should be accommodated, and the general absence of any form of man-made beauty.

Achill Island

The R319 runs westwards along the spine of the island from Achill Sound to Keel past rhododendron plantations (in flower in late spring) with **Knockmore** mountain on the south and the highest, **Slievemore**, rising to 670m (2,200ft) to the north. To the west, the peak of Croghaun is silhouetted against the mighty Atlantic Ocean. The ★★ **Atlantic Drive**, signposted to left, just beyond Achill Sound, is a stunning cliff drive before turning inland and joining up with the central R319 and continuing to **Keel**.

Atlantic Drive view

Sunset at Keel beach

At Keel there is the 3km (2-mile) stretch of golden, sandy beach. To the east of Keel are **Cathedral Rocks**. Sea action on the cliff-face has created formations in the rock not unlike splendid church vaulting.

Keem Strand, to the west of Keel, ends in the village of Dooagh. At one time basking sharks were captured off Keem Strand by local fishermen in flimsy hide-covered currachs, and brought to **Purteen Pier**, near Pol-

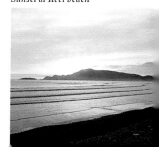

Fuschia along the N59

Ben Nephin

lagh village, for processing and export. The old tanks, used up to the 1950s to store shark oil, are still to be seen. Purteen is the main harbour for deep-sea and commercial fishing today. There are good views of Clew Bay.

Dugort, on the north shore of the island, is a small resort town with a beautiful golden strand. Nearby is the cottage used by Heinrich Böll, German writer and Nobel prize winner, whose enthusiastic *Irish Diary* written in the 1950s, has been an introduction to Ireland for many visitors. The cottage today is part of a centre for German-Irish cultural exchanges.

Return to the mainland. From Mulranny the N59 runs due north to Bangor across a great expanse of peatland with occasional patches of forestry. The inland part of County Mayo is largely covered in Atlantic blanket bog. In fine weather the bog gleams golden in the sun, and can be seen to support a varied flora, but when the sky is overcast it presents a very bleak prospect. The dark, heather-clad slopes of **Ben Nephin** (629m/2,063ft) can be seen in the east, often capped in cloud. This is a desolate, sparsely inhabited area, of comparatively monotonous countryside, lacking the charm of the Doo Lough Valley or Connemara.

From Bangor there is a 42-km (26-mile) inland route to Ballina which should be followed in bad weather. This road passes an apparently endless stretch of peatland before reaching **Bellacorick**. Here you will see huge mechanised diggers cutting up the turf, which up here is used to fire Ireland's turf-fired power station. Considering that this part of Mayo contains 1036 sq. km (400 square miles) of blanket bog it is perhaps not surprising that previous generations thought it cost effective to use it for generating electricity. Nowadays Bellacorick is supplemented by more ecologically acceptable wind turbines.

In recognition of international opinion, which advocates the conservation of such peat lands, the Irish Turf Authority, Bord na Mona, is involved in several significant conservation projects. A voluntary organisation, the **Irish Peatland Conservation Council**, has a scheme for public support whereby the purchase of a symbolic share certificates will enroll you as a 'Friend of the Bog'. Further information can be obtained from the Council at 3 Lower Mount Street, Dublin 2.

To explore **Erris** and the **Mullet** peninsula, turn left at Bangor onto the R313. The road passes the northern side of the district of Erris, a bleak, treeless area with nothing but brown heather as far as you can see. **Belmullet** is a fairly run-down town with muddy streets where efforts at urban renewal have not been successful. The best thing about it is its location on a peninsula between two wonderful land-locked bays, **Blacksod** to the south and **Broad Haven** to the north. It is something of a relief after the bleakness of Erris to see the small farmsteads, sparsely scattered maybe, but evidence at least of rural life continuing as normal. The R313 runs southwards from Belmullet to Blacksod Point. Off it are many small spur roads to piers and sandy beaches, like Elley Bay, where there is a bird sanctuary.

After returning to 'the mainland' (as it feels, even though Mullet is only a peninsula) take the left fork, the R314 for Barnatra, and follow the road signs for the ★★★ Céide Fields (mid-March to May and October, daily 10am–5pm; June to September 9.30am–6.30pm; November daily 10am–4.30pm), which appears unexpectedly on the landward side of the road as a glass cone rising out of a ridge. The award-winning three-storey structure of wood and tubular steel reveals the world of a farming community of over 5,000 years ago. Here is the single largest on-going excavation in Europe of Stone Age field system farming. Preserved under the bog, house structures, stone wall field systems and megalithic tombs cover an area of 1,000 hectares (2,500 acres). Well-designed displays and an informative audio-visual display help to make sense of the 5,000-year-old landscape. Across the road from the building is a clifftop viewing platform, very exciting if you like heights.

Many authorities consider the cliffs of north County Mayo to be one of Ireland's great undiscovered attractions. The naturalist R.L. Praeger wrote of how moved he was by this part of the country: 'the broad undulations of the treeless, roadless, moorland, the tall hills, the illimitable silver sea, the savage coastline, the booming waves, the singing wind, the smell of peat smoke and seaweed and wild thyme'.

Céide Fields

47

Stone-Age routine at Céide Fields

Downpatrick Head

Ballycastle is a small village with one sloping street. If you are interested in art, look out for the **Ballinglen Centre**, a public library with an art gallery professionally hung with exhibitions of contemporary art on a year round basis. Ballycastle is the headquarters of the Ballinglen Arts Foundation, an American-Irish initiative, which brings artists of international stature to live and work in the area, and in the process contributes to the urban renewal of a hitherto semi-derelict village.

There is a crossroads with a signpost to ★ **Downpatrick Head**. A rising walk leads along the circular rocky bay to a great piece of stratified rock severed from the cliff-face by the sea. It's a wonderful example of glacier action. Weather-permitting, you should be able to see as far as the mountains in County Sligo. The stony beach at the base of Downpatrick Head is worth exploring. Smooth layered rock formations fill with the incoming tide and make bathing pools.

The 12th-century round tower is the visible landmark of an early Christian settlement in **Killala**. Around it grew a narrow, twisting thoroughfare and as a result even the lightest traffic can create problems for this part of the quiet seaside resort. Killala is a name closely linked with the invasion of the French in 1798, who had come to assist the Irish insurgents who intended to bring an end to English rule. They first landed at nearby Kilcummin strand. On the other side of the street, St Patrick's Cathedral stands as the oldest cathedral site in the West of Ireland. Its irregular stone-work reveals the re-use of original stone from an earlier edifice. Inside, on a wall scroll, are lists of bishops from pre- and post-Reformation times. There is a lovely walk by the pier which incorporates Tír Sáile, part of Mayo's sculpture trail.

48

Experts at work in Ballina

Take the R314 south to **Ballina,** the largest town in Mayo, with a population of 7,000. Although it straddles the River Moy and has two graceful bridges, Ballina lacks architectural attractions, apart from the ruins of a 15th-century Augustinian Friary on the banks of the river at Ardnaree. It is a workaday Irish market town, albeit one with unusually bracing west coast air. It is a good place to stock up on provisions, and to eat the delicious local salmon, whether smoked or fresh. Salmon is always on the menu at the River Bar Inn, just down-river from town on the right bank of the Moy. Ballina is very popular with game anglers, who enjoy its many Edwardian and Victorian bars. The more pleasant part of the town is along the river on the Sligo road. The **Ballina Salmon Festival** takes place in July. It is a week-long celebration with street events, many for the benefit of children. There are costumed and theatrical displays, music and dancing and outdoor pageantry, and salmon from the Moy at every turn.

Ballina Salmon Festival

Route 9

Sligo Town and Yeats Country

Sligo sits calmly under the shadow of that strangely-shaped hill, Ben Bulben, remaining inimitably itself. Visitors to the West find it a pleasant change to discover a town which does not appear to make any particular effort to attract or cater for tourists. Sligo is a compact town, easy to negotiate, and visitors quickly feel part of the lively local scene. Tranquil Lough Gill offers unusual nature walks, while Rosses Point provides first class golf and Atlantic breezes. Hillsides hold a concentration of megalithic tombs. The word Sligo means 'shell', and shells and fossils abound on Sligo's beaches. It is not surprising that the famous poet William Butler Yeats found inspiration here.

W.B. Yeats was born in Dublin in 1865, son of the painter John Butler Yeats and Susan Pollexfen of Sligo. Shortly after his birth the family moved to London. Yeats' younger brother Jack was sent to live with his Pollexfen relatives in Sligo at the age of eight, and William joined him frequently for summer holidays. Jack Yeats' boyhood

Yeats's Lake Isle of Innisfree

49

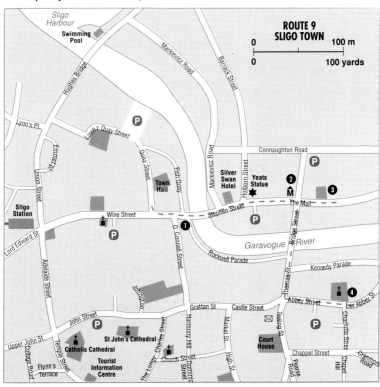

enjoyment of country scenes, travelling people, circuses and seafarers provided him with subject matter for a lifetime of painting. The **Yeats Country Drive**, a sign-posted round trip of 164km (103 miles) commemorates the achievements of both brothers. It is particularly exciting to go from the exhibition of Jack Yeats' work in Sligo town out to Rosses Point and experience the very light that he managed so successfully to paint.

W.B. Yeats

Not surprisingly, the Sligo tourist industry emphasises the early lyric work of the poet with its musical and instantly memorable lines: 'When I play on my fiddle in Dooney,/Folk dance like a wave of the sea'. But this is not enough to explain the important place W.B. Yeats has earned in Ireland as both poet and public figure. He documented the often painful process by which Ireland emerged from English rule and became a Republic: 'All changed, changed utterly:/A terrible beauty is born'. He was, in a way, the conscience of the new nation, balancing its achievements against the original romantic ideals. Later he became a senator and argued valiantly but in vain for a pluralist society in which Protestants like himself would also have a voice. His later work developed a universal philosophical depth which more than justified the Nobel prize which he was awarded in 1923. His income had always been precarious, and his first question of being told, by telephone by the editor of the Irish Times, that he had won the Nobel prize was: 'How much, Bertie, how much?'

50

Echoes of W.B. Yeats are everywhere in the Sligo area: Collooney, Ballysadare, Knocknarea, Dromahair, Dooney, Lissadell, Ben Bulben and of course the famous Lake Isle of Innisfree are all associated with his work.

Lough Gill

Nestling between a lake and the sea and encircled by mountains, ★★ **Sligo Town** is lucky in its surroundings. The **Garavogue River** runs through the town from **Lough Gill** to the sea, and was an important factor in Sligo's early prosperity. With a population of about 18,000 people, Sligo is one of the largest towns in the northwest. In the 9th century a settlement grew up here at the ford of the Garavogue. The town was developed by the Normans in the 12th century. In the latter part of the 19th century it became an important centre for trade, exporting Galway homespuns and Donegal tweeds. Among its many prosperous merchants were the Pollexfen family, from whom W.B. Yeats was descended on his mother's side.

A good place to start

The first thing to do in Sligo is to arm yourself with a copy of the poems of W.B. Yeats. There are two excellent bookshops – **Keohane's** of Castle Street, an old family-run business, and the newer **Winding Stair Bookshop and Café** near the Silver Swan Hotel.

Sligo Town

After buying your Yeats, spend some time wandering at leisure around Sligo's streets. Coming in from the wilds of northwest Mayo, it feels like a bustling hub of civilisation, while those getting off the Dublin train immediately sense a slowing of pace. Much of the town has changed little in a hundred years. Most shop-fronts in Sligo are in original old-fashioned style. Many are long-established, some family-run like the tiny bakery, Gourmet Parlour in John Street, or Tír na nÓg (land of perpetual youth) in Grattan Street, offering organic vegetables and herbal oils and spices. The Irish New Age spirit has taken quite a hold hereabouts. Michael Quirke, a butcher, turned to wood-carving and now produces Irish mythological figures which he sells in his unaltered shop in Wine Street.

Sligo Bay

Start your visit of Sligo's sights at the Silver Swan Hotel. Across the road is the **Yeats Memorial Building ❶**, a Victorian red brick former bank which is the headquarters of the annual Yeats Summer School and hosts occasional exhibitions. Since 1959 the Summer School has been held annually in August. It includes discussions by international scholars of Yeats's works, creative writing workshops, visits to places associated with the poet, and much informal socialising. A stylised bronze statue of Yeats can be seen nearby in Stephen Street.

Cross the bridge to visit ★★★ **Sligo County Museum and Library ❷** (Tuesday to Saturday 10am–1pm and 2–5pm). Located in a former chapel in Bridge Street, it contains a permanent exhibition of the paintings of Jack Yeats (1871–1957). His vigorously painted West of Ireland scenes are greatly in demand. This collection forms an excellent introduction to the work of a major Irish artist, and should not be missed. William Butler Yeats' Nobel medal and some letters are also on display.

Yeats in Stephen Street

Continue uphill along Stephen Street to the Mall to visit Sligo's **Model Arts Centre ❸**, an imposing stone school which hosts travelling exhibitions and has a busy programme of literary and musical events.

Return to Bridge Street and turn left. Among the notable well preserved and restored buildings in the town, ★ **Sligo Abbey** ❹ is the most important. Founded in 1252 by the Dominican Order, it was rebuilt after a fire in 1414. It was ruined during the sacking of Sligo in 1641. It is a and beautifully proportioned building with fine pointed windows and a tower supported on arches. The cloister also has a series of decorated arches on three sides.

Sligo Abbey

Further sights of interest include the **Court House**, a sandstone edifice built in 1878, and the **Town Hall** in Quay Street, built in 1865 in Italian Renaissance style, which can be seen from many parts of town. The oldest church is **St John's** on John Street. Designed by the German architect Richard Cassel in 1730, it has been greatly altered. It is close to the present **Catholic cathedral** of 1874, built in Romanesque Renaissance style with 69 French stained-glass windows. **Rockwell Parade**, by Douglas Hyde Bridge, is a crescent-shaped waterside development of shops and cafés and is the beginning of a walk along the river to Lough Gill. There is a waterbus stop here for trips on Lough Gill (mid-June to September).

The Town Hall

Excursions *See map on page 56*

East of Sligo

★★★ **Lough Gill**, a short walk from Sligo town, is 8km (5 miles) long and 2km (1½) miles wide. There is a signposted 38-km (24-mile) circuit of Lough Gill, part of the longer **Yeats Country Drive**. The northern bank is the most interesting. **Hazelwood Estate** has a collection of wooden sculptures by contemporary artists from Ireland and abroad arranged along an attractive forest walk.

Hazelwood sculpture

Further east along the R286 is ★★ **Parke's Castle** (May to September, daily 9.30am–6pm; October 10am–5pm), an imposing example of a 17th-century fortified manor house. It contains a great hall, with solid Irish oak beams. Spiral timber stairways lead to ramparts and towers from which there are fine views of the lake and surroundings. There is also a sallyport giving secret access to the lake. On the shore is an example of a sweathouse, an early form of sauna. There is an audio-visual display and tea rooms.

Admirers of Yeats will want to visit the Lake Isle of **Innisfree**, made famous by an early lyric poem in which the poet imagines living on the tiny island 'where peace comes dropping slow'. It is clearly signposted off the R287 before Dromahair. In summer you can hire a rowing boat and make a romantic private visit. Sensitive souls should avoid the 'water bus' that departs from Parke's Castle and encircles the island while the guide recites Yeats's poems over a loudspeaker.

This road will bring you back to Sligo past **Slish Wood** (renamed Sleuth Wood by Yeats) and **Dooney Rock**. The Rock is a designated Area of Scientific Interest with a nature trail which identifies many species of flora.

West of Sligo
Leave Sligo by John Street and take the signposted left-hand turn uphill off the R292 for ★★★ **Carrowmore megalithic cemetery** (May to September daily 9.30am–6pm), the greatest collection of stone burial tombs and circles in Ireland. While inhabitants of that age lived in temporary huts, the dead were cremated and buried with great ceremony in the tombs and chambers which we see today. A guided tour is included in admission charge.

Continue beyond Carrowmore to a crossroads with a signpost for a car park at the base of ★★ **Knocknarea Hill**. There is a narrow stony track to the summit that will take about 30 minutes to climb. Just over the ridge is a great circular stone mound said to be the burial place of **Queen Maeve** of Connacht. Measuring 192m (630ft) around its base and tapering to a height of 23m (80ft), the mound dates from 2,500BC. It provides panoramic views of the glorious Sligo landscape, including Ben Bulben and Ballysadare Bay.

Knocknarea Hill, with Queen Maeve's burial mound

53

North of Sligo
Leave town on the N15 Donegal road, turning off on the R291 at the edge of town for ★ **Rosses Point**, an attractive seaside place built on a long narrow peninsula edged by sandy beaches with a championship golf links and yacht club. Yeats and his brother Jack were among many Sligo residents who often stayed here during their summer holidays. Drop in at **Austie's Pub**, where the local fishermen drink, to savour the nautical atmosphere.

Carrowmore megalithic cemetery

Yeats's grave

118 set free

Lissadell House

Ben Bulben

Mullaghmore

Return to the N15 and continue north to **Drumcliffe** and its little churchyard. Here W.B. Yeats was re-interred in 1948, 'Under bare Ben Bulben's head', having died in France in 1939. His gravestone bears the inscription *Cast a cold eye on life, on death,/Horseman, pass by*. Also within the churchyard is a 10th-century High Cross decorated with scenes from the Gospels.

From Drumcliffe take the road to Carney for ★ **Lissadell House** (June to mid-September 10.30am–12.15pm and 2–4.15pm), a fine mansion built in 1834, still in the Gore-Booth family. Two sisters, Eva, a poet, and Constance, later Countess Markievicz, lived here at the beginning of the 20th century. Constance took part in the Easter Rising of 1916, and later became the first woman member of Dáil Eireann (Irish Parliament). The sisters were admired by Yeats (*Two girls in silk kimonos, both beautiful, one a gazelle*).

There are some excellent walks to be had in the area around Lissadell. A few miles to the west is **Raghly**, a tiny peninsula with a small harbour and a circular walk around its coast. There are good views back to Rosses Point – use the lighthouse to orient yourself. On the way to Raghly you will pass **Ardtermon Castle**, a 17th-century fortified manor house which was an earlier home of the Gore-Booths. It has been restored by a German industrialist, who for some reason painted it bright yellow, and is not open to the public.

Return to the N15 and continue north. **Sligo Crystal** has a factory shop in **Grange** where you can buy heavy cut glass of a comparable quality to Waterford crystal, at slightly reduced prices. Off nearby **Streedagh Strand**, three ships of the Spanish Armada were wrecked in 1588. Over 1,100 bodies were washed ashore. The beach is a great stretch of sand. Like much of the Sligo coast, this area is rich in fossils, which can be collected at low tide.

Continue north to **Cliffony**, where you can visit the **Creevykeel Court Tomb** (freely accessible). This is regarded as one of the finest examples of a classic court tomb in Ireland. Follow the signpost up the steps, and you will see the entrance through the end of the cairn. Archaeologists believe the burial chambers were originally covered by a corbelled roof. Excavations undertaken by a team from Harvard in 1935 dated the tomb to between 3,000 and 3,500BC.

Take the R279 to visit **Mullaghmore**, a pretty coastal village with access to several good beaches. Overlooking the harbour is Classiebawn Castle, formerly the holiday home of Lord Mountbatten who was killed here when the IRA placed a bomb on a pleasure boat that his party was using. There are good walks on Mullaghmore Head where the Atlantic waves crash onto rocky shelves.

Route 10

Boyle and its river

Inland to County Roscommon

Sligo town – Boyle – Lough Key – Carrick-on-Shannon – Strokestown – Sligo town **(148km/92 miles)** *See map, page 56*

This route travels south from Sligo on the N4 through Ballysadare and Collooney. Boyle is a pleasant, old fashioned market town on a river of the same name with a 12th-century Abbey and King House, an enormous town house which has a more than usually chequered history. The same family that owned King House also owned the land which is now Lough Key Forest Park on the southern shores of an almost circular lake. More lakes are to be found further to the east in Leitrim. Strokestown Park House and Famine Museum lies 37km (23 miles) southeast of Boyle, but is well worth the journey.

En route to Boyle, at Castlebaldwin, it is possible to take a scenic lakeside drive around **Lough Arrow**, one of Ireland's famous coarse fishing lakes. There are many islands on this lake which looks out on the Curlew Mountains.

Boyle lies at the southern foot of the Curlew Mountains on the River Boyle which connects Lough Key and Lough Gara. This is one of many places in northwest Ireland that St Patrick is reputed to have visited. Legend has it that he stumbled and fell into the River Boyle and cursed the spot where he fell. Fishing has been poor in the River Boyle ever since, but the surrounding loughs make up for it, attracting fishermen from all over the world for trout or coarse fishing and mounting numerous fishing competitions. Most of the tourists hereabouts will be in the area for the angling. Boyle itself is a pleasant little town with

Boyle: some non-angling visitors

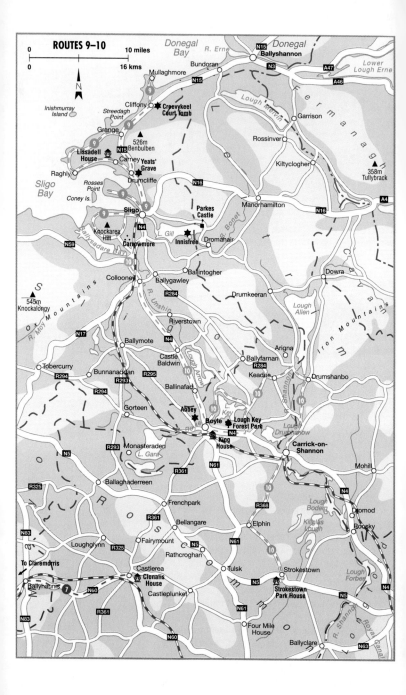

ROUTES 9–10

0 ——— 10 miles
0 ——— 16 kms

N

Donegal Bay

R. Erne

N15 *Donegal*
Ballyshannon

Mullaghmore

Lower Lough Erne

A47

A46

N3

Bundoran

N15

Lough Melvin

Cliffony

Streedagh Point

★ Creevykeel Court Tomb

Inishmurray Island

Grange

N15

526m ▲ Benbulben

F e r m a n a g h

Garrison

Rossinver

Lissadell House ⌂

Carney

Kiltyclogher

358m ▲ Tullybrack

A4

Raghly

★ Yeats' Grave

Drumcliffe

Sligo Bay

Rosses Point

Coney Is.

N16

★ Parkes Castle

Manorhamilton

N16

Sligo

9

L. Gill

★ Innisfree

Dromahair

R. Bonet

Knocknarea Hill

N4

N59

★ Carrowmore

10

Collooney

Ballintogher

Dowra

Lough Allen

Ballygawley

R. Unshin

Drumkeeran

I r o n   M o u n t a i n s

Riverstown

R284

N17

Ballymote

N4

Castle Baldwin

Lough Arrow

Arigna

Ballyfarnan

R284

Tobercurry

Bunnanaddan

R295

10

Keadue

Drumshanbo

R294

R293

Ballinafad

Shannon

10

Gorteen

★ Abbey

Key

10

Lough Drumharlow

545m ▲ Knockalongy

Ox M o y   Mountains

R. Moy

R294

R293

★ Boyle

Lough Key Forest Park

N4 King House

Carrick-on-Shannon

Monasteraden

L. Gara

N4

Mohill

N5

R361

N61

N4

R325

Ballaghaderreen

Frenchpark

R368

Lough Boderg

Dromod

10

Elphin

N61

Killglas Lough

Boosky

Bellangare

R361

Fairymount

N5

N83

Loughglynn

R325

Rathcroghan

Tulsk

N5

Strokestown

Lough Forbes

10

N61

R325

To Claremorris

Ballyhaunis

7

N60

Castlerea ⌂ Clonalis House

Castleplunket

13 Strokestown Park House

N5

R. Shannon

N83

R361

N60

Four Mile House

N61

Ballyclare

N63

Royal Canal

an old-fashioned air about it. Perched on the bridge, the **Royal Hotel**, dating from about 1770 with its distinctive Tudor-like facade, is the social hub of the place with a busy bar, coffee shops and an attractive restaurant overlooking a narrow stretch of the river.

On the north edge of the town, also by the river, are the impressive ruins of the ★ **Boyle Abbey** (mid-June to mid-September, daily 10am–6pm), a Cistercian abbey. Founded in 1161, and consecrated in 1218, the abbey is a perfect example of the transitional period when Irish ecclesiastical architecture was changing from Romanesque to Gothic style. The arches on the north side of its long nave are pointed Gothic arches, while on the southern side they are rounded and Romanesque. Carvings of grotesque beasts and human figures can still be seen in the nave. The buildings were damaged in the Elizabethan wars, and from the 16th century until the end of the 18th century the abbey was used as a fort. There is a reconstruction of the original design in the abbey's renovated gate house.

Boyle Abbey

★ **King House** (May to September, Tuesday to Sunday 10am–6pm; October and April, weekends 10am–6pm) is an imposing stone mansion standing at the east end of the main street, which was originally designed as an avenue leading up to it. A large three-storey over basement residence with a central block and two projecting wings, it was built for Sir Henry King, MP, about 1730. His son Edward King, inherited a baronetcy and by 1768 had been elevated to Earl of Kingston. It is one of the finest examples of a town house of its period, although it was several times almost lost to posterity, as an exhibit inside will explain. The house has a long narrow hall, with 11 window bays along the garden front. Rooms on all four floors have vaulted ceilings. It is hard to imagine one family living in a house on such a scale, and indeed the King family did not stay here for long; after only 50 years they moved out to a new house, Rockingham, on the shores of Lough Key. King House subsequently became an army barracks for the Connaught Rangers, then for the Irish army, and then was allowed to fall derelict. A series of exhibits inside illustrates the history of the house, of the Connaught Rangers and of the Kings of Connacht. The colourful history of the King family brings that period of Anglo-Irish history known as the Ascendancy vividly to life. The family died out shortly after its other house, Rockingham, burnt down in 1957. Boyle's adventurous civic art collection, which features contemporary Irish art, is housed on the ground floor of the building. There is also a coffee shop, and the tourist office for the area.

57

King House: the salon

Frybrook House (June to September, daily 2–6pm), at the other end of Boyle, gives a more modest picture of

Lough Key

18th-century living. The house belonged to an English Quaker who came to Boyle at the invitation of the Earl of Kingston to establish a weaving community. The house, which was built around 1752, has been extensively restored. It also offers B&B (tel: 079/62170).

Family outing to Lough Key Forest Park

The N4 east of out of Boyle leads to **Lough Key Forest Park** (daily all year; admission fee Easter to September), which occupies a lakeside demesne, granted during Cromwellian times (1617) to the King family, and held by them until 1957. The Forest and Wild Life Service now run the 350-hectare (800-acre) park. Rockingham House, designed by Robert Nash on a similarly grand scale to King House, was lost by fire in 1957. The Ice House, and a subterranean passage used to keep staff and tradesmen out of sight of the family, still stand near the lake. The neoclassical stable block also remains, along with the chapel and a picturesque 18th-century folly in the shape of a temple. The islands on the 5-km (3-mile) wide lake have remains of medieval monasteries. Boats, rowing or motor, can be hired from the quay beside the 1960s rustic restaurant building. There are also organised guided boat trips (July and August). A viewing tower called the Moylurg Tower, built of concrete blocks in a style best described as brutalist, is visible from all points. In general Lough Key feels more like a bizarre city park than a part of the wild west of Ireland. The gardens have signposted walks on wide gravel paths and feature many of the ornamental trees planted in the 18th century, and a Bog Garden with a wide range of rhododendrons and azaleas. Cairns, ring forts and a court cairn can also be seen.

Moylung Tower

The perfect antidote to the municipal park atmosphere of the Forest Park can be found nearby among the lakes of **Leitrim**. Return to the N4 and head towards Boyle, ignoring the turn off for the town. After about a mile turn right for **Corrigeenroe** (start of the scenic drive around Lough Key), then follow signs for **Keadue**, an unusually pretty village backed by the Arigna Mountains. Here take the R285 for **Drumshanbo**, a pleasant village on the shores of Lough Allen with several good pubs. Lough Allen forms part of the mighty river Shannon. **Carrick-on-Shannon**, 13km (8 miles) to the south on the R207, is the main base for pleasure craft and anglers. Besides having a marina full of cruisers which can be rented by the week, Carrick also has a lively pub and restaurant scene.

From Carrick-on-Shannon, take the R368 south for 14km (9 miles) to Elphin, and from there a further 11km (7 miles) to the village of **Strokestown**. With its wide main street, Strokestown was supposedly modelled on the *Ring Strasse* in Vienna, and was laid out in the early 19th century to complement the new Gothic entrance to ★★ **Strokestown Park House** (May to September, Tuesday to Sunday 11.30am–5.30pm; 40-minute guided tour only). A fine Palladian mansion designed by Richard Cassels in the 1730s, the house originally formed the centrepiece of a 2,500-hectare (6,000-acre) estate. The central three-storey block with a pillared portico is linked by curving corridors to the wings, one of which contains the stables. The guided tour is relentlessly chatty and explains the house's history and curiosities. There is a gallery above the kitchen from which the lady of the house would drop a menu on the Monday morning with instructions for the week's meals. There is also a fully equipped nursery wing and a distillery. The last of the Mahon family, Mrs Olive Hayes Pakenham Mahon, lived here more or less in one room until 1979, when she sold both house and what was left of the park to a local businessman, who is responsible for the restoration. Consequently most of the furniture and equipment are original, and the house retains an atmospheric, lived-in feeling, even if some corners are shabby in comparison with more formally restored properties.

Strokestown Park House

59

The ★★★ **Famine Museum** (hours as above, additional admission fee), which is housed in the stable yard, presents an award-winning documentary exhibition of the famine years of the mid-19th century based on state archives and the Strokestown Estate records. The lively, detailed and well-balanced exhibition explains the political, economic and natural events the produced the Great Famine and emigration, and draws parallels with conditions in the Third World in the 20th century. Allow at least an hour for the museum. There is a pleasant coffee shop adjoining the museum. The walled garden (separate admission fee) has only recently been replanted, and needs time to mature.

Famine Museum

The Historic Landscape

Opposite: Carrowmore megalithic cemetery

The West of Ireland is famed for the wild beauty of its landscape. But even a rugged wilderness area bears traces of Man's intervention. The blanket bog that covers much of the West has been harvested as fuel since medieval times. Even today you will see people in the summer months, cutting turf with the traditional sharp, narrow spade known as a sleán, and leaving it to dry in the sun. It is then carried home and stacked beside the back door for use as winter fuel. In places up to 3m (12ft) of turf have been dug away over the years, and it was because of this that the settlement dating from 5,000BC known as the Céide Fields was first discovered.

Reconstructed peat and thatch house, Ballina

Under the blanket bog of North Mayo at the Céide Fields (*see Route 8*) you can see the remains of the houses and the walls of the farming people living near these cliffs over 50 centuries ago. The stones were not quarried, but were lifted off the land where they had been deposited during the last Ice Age. Dry stone walls are still used extensively today as field divisions.

Life in Céide Fields

61

Neolithic tombs dating from about 4,000BC, like the Poulnabrone dolmen in the Burren (*see Route 8*), were usually placed in commanding positions on hill tops. While these tombs obviously formed part of a funeral rite, nothing more is known about them. Traces of numerous ring, earth and promontory forts dating from the Iron Age to Early Christian times can also be seen. Dun Aengus on the Aran Islands (*see Route 3*) is one of the finest. These were fortified homesteads into which cattle were herded in times of danger. The dwellings within the forts were built on the post-and-wattle technique, and remained a normal place of habitation down to medieval times.

Dun Aengus fort

Christianity arrived in Ireland in the mid 5th century. Remains of early Christian oratories built of stone with corbelled roofs can be seen on the Aran Islands. It was not until the Norman invasion in the 12th century that a recognisably European type of ecclesiastical architecture was introduced. The Normans were also responsible for the introduction of castles. The original Norman castles were essentially fortified homes with massively thick walls. Like Dunguaire Castle in Kinvara (*see Route 4*), castles were usually sited on high ground near a source of fresh water. You will quickly learn to tell a genuinely old castle from an imitation like Ashford Castle in Cong, which dates only from the late 19th century.

There is a distinct lull in architectural activity in the West of Ireland between the destructive suppression of the 1641 Rebellion by the parliamentary army, in which many churches and abbeys were ruined, and the early 19th century. With the exception of the centre of Limerick city (*see*

Route 1) and the occasional grand country House like Glin Castle (*see Route 1*) and Westport House (*see Route 6*), the celebrated Georgian architecture of the 18th century is largely absent.

Population growth in the first half of the 19th century was phenomenal. Over 1,550,000 people were living in the area from County Clare up to Sligo, many of them totally dependent on the potato crop. Compare that to the figure today of about 500,000. It is still easy to spot small ridged fields on steep sloping mountainsides – evidence that potatoes were cultivated there. A catastrophe was inevitable. Around one third of the population either died during the famine years of 1845–8, or emigrated to the New World. The full story is told in the Famine Museum at Strokestown Park House (*see Route 10*).

The economic depression that followed lasted well into the 20th century. It is only in the last 40 years that the West has started to prosper. The preferred style of domestic architecture is no longer the traditional Irish cottage. Cottages are still associated with poverty and backwardness, and people prefer to build in a more exotic style, often referred to as 'Spanish hacienda'. One of the most blatant instances of inappropriate development is along the once-scenic R336 Spiddal–Rossaveale road outside Galway city. In recent years planning law has been more stringently enforced, and domestic architecture is improving. Another scenic blight which many people deplore are the rafts that indicate the presence of fish and shell fish farming, which have sprung up even in the beautiful Killary Harbour. Like many tourist destinations that depend on their wilderness appeal, the West of Ireland is having to seek a balance between the livelihood of its permanent residents, and the expectations in terms of unspoilt scenery of its many visitors.

Traditional Cottage on Inishere

Hacienda-style B&B

Achill Island

The Arts in the West

Considering its small population, the West of Ireland makes a disproportionately large contribution to the Irish arts scene. Because of the survival of the Irish language in the region, it is not surprising that the West has a unique and important place in traditional Irish culture. What is perhaps unexpected is the large contribution made by the West to the Irish arts scene overall – producing or nurturing playwrights, poets, visual artists, film-makers and pop music groups who are as cosmopolitan and contemporary in outlook as their colleagues in Dublin, London or New York.

Galway City is undoubtedly the capital of the Irish traditional music world. Traditional music thrives in the West's informal pub scene. If there is a *fleadh* (traditional music festival) in town, musicians will come from far and near to listen to the big names and to participate in informal sessions. Kinvara in Co. Galway, Ennis in Co. Clare, and in July and August, Doolin and the whole coast of west Clare, are also important musical centres.

Players in Sligo

63

Set dancing in Kinvara

Much instrumental Irish music is dance music – jigs, reels, hornpipes, polkas and so on. Until well into this century, dancing was the most popular form of entertainment in the West. Set dancing, which is a cross between Irish step dancing and the quadrille (similar to American barn dancing), has experienced a phenomenal revival in the West over the past 20 years, having almost died out. Dances are once again held in the open air at crossroads, and many pubs offer informal lessons.

Given all this musical activity, it is not surprising that the West of Ireland has also produced major successes in the pop scene. The Saw Doctors, for example, are originally from Tuam, Co. Galway, while Dolores O'Riordan and the Cranberries are from Limerick.

The first wave of Irish intellectuals to discover the West were those involved in the Celtic Revival at the turn of the century. The poet W.B. Yeats (*see Route 9*) was from Sligo on his mother's side, and eventually owned a rural retreat near Gort, Co. Galway. It was Yeats who first suggested to the playwright John Millington Synge (1871–1909) that he visit the Aran Islands. Synge's masterpiece, *The Playboy of the Western World*, is still performed regularly today, and was one of the early successes, back in 1982, of the Galway-based theatre company, Druid. Druid tour regularly to the US, Australia and the UK. One of their recent triumphs was a co-production with London's Royal Court Theatre of *The Leenane Trilogy*, three plays set in Connemara written by a young London-Irish playwright, Martin McDonagh. For a tragi-comic warts-and-all portrait of present day Connemara, the trilogy is hard to beat.

*Druid Theatre and
Leenane Trilogy performance*

Nowadays Druid shares Galway's new Town Hall Theatre with another local company, Punchbag, and with visiting touring companies. Macnas, a Galway-based troupe of performance artists, have gained wide acclaim and are also greatly in demand abroad. Galway's fourth resident theatre company is An Taibhearc, the national Irish-language theatre, which puts on an annual summer show that can be enjoyed by non-Irish speakers.

Irish film-making has come a long way from the stage-Irishness of *The Quiet Man*, filmed in 1952 at Cong in Co. Mayo (*see Route 7*). The Galway Film Fleadh, an annual event which premieres work by Irish directors as well as by international film-makers, is important both for viewing and for informal networking. On the Aran Islands during the summer, look out for showings of Robert O'Flaherty's famous 1934 documentary classic *Man of Aran*, a record of the islander's struggle with the sea.

While there are numerous first rate artists living and working in the West of Ireland – Seán MacSweeney and Barrie Cooke in Sligo, Camille Souter on Achill, Brian Bourke and John Behan in Galway, Eddie Delaney in Carraroe – it is not always easy for the visitor to see their work. Delaney has established his own open-air sculpture park at Carraroe, but Galway lacks a proper gallery, while Sligo, (whose Jack Yeats collection is a must for art lovers) makes do with a converted church and a converted school.

In art, as in literature, numerous practitioners take inspiration from the West without actually living there. Because the West is seen by the Irish a place for spiritual regeneration and rediscovery of roots, it frequently forms the occasional subject matter of poets living elsewhere in the country – from the bitterly comic Paul Durcan to the metaphysical Derek Mahon and the mystical Richard Murphy, who lived for a long time on Inishbofin. Novelists are less likely to set their work in rural parts these days. Modern Irish fiction was dominated by novels set in the country – for example, the work of County Clare-born Edna O'Brien – right up until the arrival of the latest generation of street-wise Dubliners, led by Roddy Doyle. A backlash against rural themes was perhaps inevitable, but may not last forever.

There is a lively poetry scene in the West. International names join the locals at annual literary festivals held in Galway and Sligo, and at the many summer schools. Poetry readings are held year-round and tend to be informal affairs, often in a pub. Galway's Rita Ann Higgins, a witty working class voice, is an act to look out for, as is Dermot Healy, who often reads to the accompaniment of traditional musicians. The great W.B. Yeats, who read solemnly in a kind of chant, may or may not have approved.

Calendar of Events

March
Saint Patrick's Day Parade, Galway City.

April
Limerick's Irish Film Festival. A showcase for Irish film-makers. **Cuirt International Poetry Festival** is a four day weekend with readings by Irish and international poets, and workshops.

May
Fleadh Nua, Ennis, Co. Clare. Major Irish folk music festival with organised and impromptu street and pub sessions. **Sligo Arts Festival**. A lively celebration including theatre, parades, fireworks, comedy, readings and music.

Festival season

July
Siamsa (Folk theatre) Taibhdhearc Theatre, Galway city. Irish mime, song and dance. **Willie Clancy Summer School**, Milltown Malbay, Co. Clare. A week-long celebration with traditional music and dancing. **Archaeological Summer School**, Wavecrest Hotel, Dooagh, Achill, Co. Mayo. For enthusiasts who want to learn techniques of surveying, excavation and draughtsmanship. **Galway Arts Festival**, Galway city. Major international event with theatre, music, exhibitions, and street theatre, followed immediately by the **Galway Races**, another festive week.

August
Cruinniú na mBád (Gathering of the Boats), Kinvara, Co. Galway. A week of racing with traditional craft which attracts the cream of traditional musicians and singers. **Yeats International Summer School**, Hawk's Well Theatre, Sligo. Leading international academics gather for seminars and poetry workshops, combined with tours of Yeats Country. **Merriman Summer School**, Falls Hotel, Ennistymon, Co. Clare. Discussions of Irish history and politics by day, Irish entertainment by night.

September
Clarinbridge Oyster Festival, Co. Galway. The original festival is still held at Paddy Burke's pub in Clarinbridge at the start of the month. A second three-day Oyster Festival is held in Galway city at the end of the month. **Clifden Arts Week**, Co. Galway. Music and readings organised by the Clifden community. **Matchmaking Festival**, Lisdoonvarna, Co. Clare. A light-hearted week of old time dancing aimed at mature singles, continuing the tradition in which farmers came to Lisdoonvarna when the harvest was in to look for a wife.

Clarinbridge Oyster festival

Food and Drink

The great bonus of the food available in the West of Ireland lies in the high quality of the fresh local produce. Galway is considered the best place in Ireland for salmon. Be sure to try locally smoked salmon, as well as fresh. Lobster, prawns, scallops, mussels and sole are all fished on this coast. The Galway oyster beds are famous too. At the opening of the new season in September every pub for miles around serves fresh oysters with brown soda bread, butter, and pints of Guinness.

Irish soda bread, a yeast-free bread made from stone-ground wheat flour, buttermilk and soda bicarbonate is a staple in the west of Ireland. Still made daily in many homes, good versions are also available commercially.

The other great treat in the West is locally produced lamb. Rack of lamb is usually cooked to order, and can be eaten pink or, as the Irish would say, underdone. The cheaper cuts are used in Irish stew, a creamy combination of lamb braised with onion, carrots and potato flavoured with parsley and thyme. Local beef is also excellent, whether served as char-grilled steaks or braised in Guinness. In the winter pheasant and venison appear on the more upmarket menus. Potatoes are eaten with every meal, and may appear in two or more guises – boiled in their skins, *and* mashed or chipped. The West is not a good area for salads, given its damp climate. The best chefs grow their own herbs and salads.

Restaurants in the West are predominately small and informal. Even the most elegant country house hotels ask for no more than 'jacket and tie' after six. Many of the smaller establishments are run by an owner-chef. Galway has a lively dining-out scene with a more cosmopolitan ambience than other towns. Ennis, Doolin, Ballyvaughan, Kinvara, Clifden, Westport and Sligo all offer a choice of good restaurants and bar food.

Wine is now widely available, but the drink to try hereabouts is stout, the most famous of which is Guinness. Always poured with great care, it can take a good five minutes for your pint to be ready. But the result, smooth as velvet, will be worth the wait. Irish coffee – hot sweet black coffee containing a measure of whiskey, topped with whipped cream – is generally served at the end of a meal, but in cold, wet weather it can be a great mid-morning or mid-afternoon 'livener'. *Sláinte*!

Bar food

The biggest innovation in recent years has been the widespread introduction of bar food at both lunchtime and early evening. If you have eaten an Irish breakfast – cereal followed by bacon, egg, sausage, black and white puddings

67

Pints in hand in Ballina

Traditional Irish produce

Gus O'Connor's

and tomato, with toast and soda bread – you are unlikely to want a big lunch. Bar food options include sandwiches and salads, soups and seafood chowder, and also hot dishes of the day like Irish stew, beef in Guinness, plaice and chips or roast meat and vegetables. In the evening the menu might be extended. Most pubs also serve tea and coffee during the day. Note, however, that publicans like to revert to their main business of selling drink by around 9pm. Tipping is not expected in bars, even when you are eating.

Some of the best places for bar food are: **The Monk's Pub**, Ballyvaughan; **Noctan's**, Cross Street in Galway city; **Gus O'Connor's**, Doolin; **The Cloister**, Ennis; **Austie's**, Rosses Point; **Hargadon's**, Sligo; and **The Asgard** and **The Tower Bar** on Westport's quays. **Paddy Burke's** in Clarinbridge and **Moran's of the Weir** in nearby Kilcolgan both specialise in Galway oysters.

Seafood restaurant near Galway

Restaurant Selection

The following is a list of restaurants along the suggested tour routes in the West of Ireland. Cost categories as follows: **£££** = expensive, **££** = moderate, **£** = inexpensive.

Ballyvaughan
Gregan's Castle Hotel, Corkscrew Hill, tel: 065/770055. Country house hotel overlooking the Burren offering French cuisine in an elegant dining room where a harpist often plays. Closed November to March. £££.

Bunratty
MacCloskey's Restaurant, Bunratty House Mews, tel: 061/364802. Sophisticated cuisine featuring fresh local produce, including game in season, served in the atmospheric basement of the 17th-century Bunratty House. Closed February. £££.

Clifden
O'Grady's Seafood, Market Street, tel:095/21450. Cosy, town centre restaurant, with a good reputation for seafood, and a great choice of desserts. Closed November to mid-March. ££. **Rock Glen Manor**, Ballyconneely Road, tel: 095/21035. A 19th-century shooting lodge has been converted into a charming, informal country house hotel. The restaurant has an adventurous modern menu using fresh local produce. Closed November to mid-March. ££.

Doolin
Bruach na Haille, tel: 065/74120. Cheerful cottage restaurant with stone flagged floor and brightly laden pine dressers offering an unpretentious menu featuring Irish specials like steak with whiskey sauce, and plenty of fresh seafood. Closed November to mid-March. ££.

Ennis
The Cloister , Abbey Street, tel: 065/29521. Built within the walls of a 13th-century abbey, this is an atmospheric spot with low-ceilinged rooms and open fires, serving an imaginative menu with a good range of seafood. ££.

Galway
McDonagh's Fish Restaurant. Kirwan's Lane, tel: 091/565001. For many years a wet fish shop with a few tables, McDonagh's is now a fully-fledged classic seafood restaurant, and the best place to try Galway oysters. £££. (Their adjacent fish and chip bar serves a wide choice of battered fish with chips. £.) **Nimmo's**, Spanish Arch, tel: 091-653565. First floor restaurant in an old stone building beside the River Corrib just beyond the Spanish Arch. Swiss chef Stephan Zeltner serves a robust menu featuring plenty of alcohol and cream. £££. **The Malt House**, Olde Malte Arcade, High Street, tel: 091/563993. Chintzy pub restaurant with white rough cast walls tucked away in an alley. A place for old reliables like duckling à l'orange, steak or fresh prawns pan fried in garlic butter. ££.

Nimmo's Wine Bar

Kinvara
Merriman Inn, tel: 091/638222. This spacious restaurant in a modern thatched hotel is run by one of Ireland's leading chefs, Michael Clifford, known for imaginative interpretations of traditional dishes. Try his wild Irish salmon with champ (mashed potatoes and spring onions). ££.

Lisdoonvarna
The Orchid Room, Sheedy's Spa View Hotel, tel: 065/74026. Hidden away in a family-run hotel is one of West Clare's outstanding restaurants, where the owner's son, Frankie, cooks local produce in a seriously accomplished style. Closed October to March. ££.

Moycullen
Drimcong House, tel: 091/555115. This elegant restaurant in a 300-year-old lakeside house 13km (8 miles) west of Galway city is the base of *chef extraordinaire*, Gerry Galvin. Book in advance for a memorable gastronomic experience. Closed December 25 to mid-March. £££.

Westport
The Asgard Restaurant, The Quay, Westport Quay, tel: 098/25319. Long-established restaurant above a quayside bar with an unpretentious menu emphasising fresh local produce. ££. **Quay Cottage Restaurant**, The Harbour, tel:098/26412. Old cottage converted into a nautically-themed restaurant. Fish and seafood features strongly, but meat-eaters and vegetarians also catered for. ££.

The Asgard Restaurant

Riding near the Cliffs of Moher

Connemara ponies

Active Holidays

Riding

A variety of residential riding holidays are available for both children and adults, while many local stables offer riding by the hour or half-day. Connemara ponies are used alongside sturdy Irish hunter types and quiet cobs. Stables offer either trekking (suitable for beginners) or hacking (some experience desirable) from about £12 per hour. The **Ashford Equestrian Centre** (Cong, Co. Mayo, tel: 092/46507, fax: 092/46024) offers trekking and hacking, cross-country riding and instruction in the indoor arena. Accommodation can be arranged with local B&Bs or in self-catering cottages. The **Galway–Clare–Burren Trail** (Ballycrissane, Portumna, Co. Galway, tel: 0905/75205, fax 75247) is a six-day post-to-post trail passing a wide variety of landscapes from beach to bog and forest, finishing on the famous Cliffs of Moher. Baggage is transported, and accommodation is arranged in hotels or B&Bs. The **Horse Holiday Farm** (Mount Temple, Grange, Co. Sligo, tel: 071/66152, fax: 66400) runs a similar operation through equally interesting scenery in Sligo.

Golf

Golfing facilities are extensive, with championship and nine-hole courses. Top courses include: **Lahinch**, Co. Clare, tel: 065/81003 (links, par 72); **Dromoland**, Newmarket on Fergus, Co. Clare, tel: 061/368144 (parkland, par 71); **Galway Bay Golf and Country Club**, Renville, Oranmore, Co. Galway, tel: 091/790500 (parkland with sea views, par 72); **Westport Golf Club**, Carrowholly, Westport, Co. Mayo, tel: 098/25113 (parkland, par 73); **Connemara Isles Golf Club**, Eanach Mhéain, Leitir moír, Connemara, Co. Galway, tel: 091/72498 (links, par 70);

Enniscrone Golf Club, Co. Sligo, tel: 096/36297 (links, par 72). Trolleys can be hired locally but bring your own clubs. Green fees start from IR£18 and average IR£25 depending on day of the week and season.

Walking and Cycling

Walking and cycling holidays can be organised for groups and individuals. Organisers provide itineraries, guide, accommodation, transfer of luggage and cycle hire. Specialists include: **Connemara Tourism**, Letterfrack, Co. Galway, tel: 095/43950; **Burren Walking Holidays**, Carrigann Hotel, Lisdoonvarna, Co. Clare, tel: 065/74036; **Geotreks**, 13 Carrowbeg Estate, Westport, Co. Mayo, tel: 098/28702. The cost of the holiday will depend largely on the category of accommodation.

Cycle hire on Clare Island

Angling

Counties Mayo, Galway, Clare and Sligo offer excellent facilities for anglers. Whether deep-sea, coarse or game fishing, the choice of locations and species is wide.

A welcome sign

Fully equipped deep-sea fishing boats are located at Clifden, Roundstone, Cleggan, Letterfrack and Spiddal – all in Co. Galway. There are also boats at Killala, Belmullet, Achill, Newport and Westport in Co. Mayo and along the Clare coast at Kilrush, Doolin, Doonbeg and Liscannor. Deep-sea boats cater for up to 12 anglers and cost about £20 per person for a full day charter. The season runs from April to October. The Irish Tourist Board publishes three brochures on Game Angling, Sea Angling and Coarse Fishing which give information on the seasons, fisheries, licences and permits. It also gives details of a number of hotels and guest houses in Galway and Mayo that offer week-long seminars with practical instructions in every aspect of casting and fishing. Details can also be obtained from Tourist Information Offices or by contacting the **Western Regional Fisheries Board**, Weir Lodge, Earls Island, Galway, tel: 091/563118, fax: 566335.

71

Angling at Ballynahinch

Diving

Underwater visibility for sub-aqua divers along the West coast averages 12 metres. There is an abundance of sea life. Further information can be obtained from the **Irish Underwater Council**, 78a Patrick Street, Dun Laoghaire, Co. Dublin, tel: 01 284 4601.

Surfing

Notable surfing venues are found at Strandhill and Easkey, Co. Sligo, and at Lahinch, Kilkee, and Spanish Point, Co. Clare. Further details are available from the **Irish Surfing Association** is at Easkey House, Easkey, Co. Sligo, tel: (096) 49020.

Getting There

Opposite: life in the slow lane

By Air

Shannon Airport (tel: 061 471444) is the main gateway to the West. Aer Lingus operate flights to Shannon from London Heathrow; AB Airlines from Gatwick, Stanstead and Birmingham; and British Airways Express from Manchester. Aer Lingus also has flights to Shannon from Boston, Chicago, New York and Newark; Delta Airlines from New York and Atlanta; and Aeroflot from New York, Chicago and Washington. These and other carriers also operate charter flights during the summer. There are daily flights from Dublin to Shannon, and also from Dublin to **Galway Airport** (tel: 091 752874). **Knock International Airport**, (tel: 094 67222) receives daily flights from Stanstead with Ryanair; from Manchester with British Airways Express; and from Birmingham with Aer Lingus.

The terminal at Knock

By Rail

Irish Rail (Iarnrod Eireann), tel: (01) 836 62222, provides daily connections between Dublin and towns in the West. Heuston Station, Dublin serves Limerick, Galway, Westport and Ballina; Connolly Station serves Boyle and Sligo.

73

By Coach

National Express (Eurolines) in Britain, in conjunction with Bus Eireann, operate daily coach services between Britain and Ireland – British enquiries, tel: (0990) 808080.

Bus Eireann operate daily services from Bus Áras (central bus station) in Store Street, Dublin, to all towns and cities in the West. Enquiries, tel: (01) 836 6111.

By sea

Irish Ferries (tel: 0171-499 5744) provide daily sailings between Holyhead and Dublin and between Pembroke in Wales and Rosslare on the south coast. Stena Line (tel: 01233 624 7022) operates its HSS (High Speed Service) several times daily between Holyhead and Dun Laoghaire, as well as conventional services between Holyhead and Dublin and between Fishguard and Rosslare.

Stena Line HSS at Dun Laoghaire

By car

Dublin or Dun Laoghaire are the most convenient ports for those travelling on by car to the West. Leave Dublin on the M4/N4 for the West. In Kinnegad, fork left onto the N6 for Galway or keep on the N4 for Sligo, turning off in Longford on to the N5 for Castlebar, Westport and Ballina. If travelling from Dublin to Limerick or Co. Clare, take the N7. Dublin to Galway is 272km (169 miles), to Sligo 214km (133 miles) and to Westport 257km (160 miles). Dublin to Limerick is 193km (120 miles).

Loaded up for the West

Getting Around

Sightseeing bus in Galway

By bus

Long distance bus routes, operated by Bus Eireann, are well-developed. In summer extra bus routes are provided, especially on the west coast. Travel costs are about half the equivalent trip by train, though the journey can often take longer. Various special fares are available. The Rambler ticket enables one to travel throughout the national network for periods of three, eight or 15 days.

Taxi and Hackney

There are metered taxis at railway stations in Limerick, Galway and Sligo. Elsewhere, fares are agreed with the driver in advance. In cities and towns you can book a taxi by telephone. Look in the *Golden Pages* classified telephone directory under 'Taxis'.

Uncongested Doolin

By car

Driving can still be a real pleasure in the West of Ireland, as the roads are the least congested in Europe. Drive on the left is the rule, although there is a predilection in some rural areas for the middle of the road. Drivers and front-seat passengers must wear seat belts. The speed limit is either 30 mph (48 kph), 40 mph (64kph) or 50 mph (80kph) in urban areas, 60 mph (97 kph) on country roads, with 70 mph (112 kph) permitted on motorways.

Car hire

At the height of summer, hire cars can be hard to find, so book in advance. In the West, the smaller the car, the better – the most alluring lanes are the narrowest. You must be over 23 with two year's full licence and under 76 to hire a car.

Avis, Dublin Airport, tel: 605 7555; Shannon Airport, tel: 061-471094; Galway, tel: 091-568886.

Budget Rent-a-Car, Dublin Airport, tel: 844 5919; Shannon Airport, tel: 061-471688; Galway, Eyre Square, tel: 091-566376.

Dan Dooley Rent-a-Car, Dublin Airport, tel: 844 5156; Shannon Airport, tel: 061-471098.

Diplomat Cars, Knock Airport, tel: 094-67252.

Eurodollar, Arrivals hall, Dublin Airport, tel: 260 3371; Shannon Airport, tel: 061-472633.

Hamill's Rent-a-Car, Mullingar, tel: 044-48682/44500. Delivery to Dublin, Shannon and Knock airports.

Hertz Rent-a-Car, Dublin Airport, tel: 844 5488; Shannon Airport, tel: 061-471369.

Murrays Europcar Rent-a-Car, Dublin Airport, tel: 844 4179; Shannon Airport, tel: 061-471618; Galway, tel: 091-562222; Knock Airport, tel: 0778-33029.

Cycle hire

Raleigh Rent-a-Bike, based at Kylemore Road, Dublin 10, tel: 01-626 1333, offers a system of pick-up at one place and return to another. Bicycles can be hired by the day or the week in most major towns in the West.

Ferries to the Aran Islands

Several ferry companies serve the islands, and competition is lively. Look out for good deals when you book, including family and group tickets, a night's accommodation free or greatly reduced, or a return trip by air. Tickets are not transferable between the rival ferry companies, so make sure you know your ferry's timetable before you go ashore.

Aran Island connections

The busiest port for the Aran Islands is **Rossaveale**, 32km/20 miles west of Galway. There are regular bus connections from Galway for an extra £3. Parking at Rossaveale is free but unsupervised.

Island Ferries, Victoria Place, Eyre Square, Galway, tel: 091/561767 serve the islands year round from Rossaveale for about £15 return. The crossing takes 20–45 minutes depending on the size of the boat and the weather conditions. **Aran Ferries** are based at the Galway Tourist Information Office (*see page 76*). From June to September they have daily sailings from the Galway Docks, a 90-minute crossing for about £16 return. **Aer Árann** (tel: 091/593034) are based at Inverin west of Spiddal. They fly daily to all three islands for about £35 return. If you are planning to visit Inishere, the shortest crossing – about 40 minutes on a small, open boat – is from Doolin in Co. Clare, with the **Doolin Ferry Co.**, tel: 065/74455 (mid-April to September).

Glossary

All road signs are in Irish

In the Irish-speaking part of South Connemara all road signs are in Irish. Good road maps show the names in both Irish and English. If you familiarise yourself with the following list, you should have no trouble.

Gaillimh	Galway	*Sraith Salach*	Recess
An Spidéal	Spiddal	*An Caiseal*	Cashel
Indreabhán	Inverin	*An Clochán*	Clifden
R-Inverin	Rossaveale	*Oileáin Arainn*	Aran Islands
An Cheathrú	Carraroe	*Inis Mn*	Inishmore
Maigh Cuilinn	Moycullen	*Inis Meáin*	Inishmaan
Uachtar Ard	Oughterard	*Inis Oírr*	Inishere
An Teach Dard	Maam Cross		

Other essential Irish, extensively used on toilets (*Leithreas*): *Fir* - Gents, *Mná* - Ladies.

Facts for the Visitor

Emergency

For **emergency services**, such as police, ambulance, fire service, lifeboat and coastal rescue, tel: 999 and ask for the service you need.

Medical services

Medical insurance is highly advisable for all visitors. However, visitors from EU countries are entitled to medical treatment in Ireland, North and South, under a reciprocal arrangement.

With the exception of UK citizens, visitors from EU states should obtain form E111 from their own national social security office. These forms entitle the holders to free treatment by a doctor and free medicines on prescription. If hospital treatment is necessary, this will be given free in a public ward. UK visitors need only go to a doctor (or, in an emergency, a hospital), present some proof of identity (e.g. driving licence) and request treatment under the EU health agreement.

To find a doctor either ask your hotel to recommend one or contact the Regional Health Board listed in the local phone directory's 'green pages'.

Tipping

Taxi drivers expect 10 to 15 per cent of the fare. Waiters in restaurants expect the same tip wherever menus say 'service not included'. Bar staff in pubs are not tipped as a rule, even if they are serving bar food.

Service with a smile

Tourist information

For information on Ireland contact the offices of the **Irish Tourist Board** (Bord Fáilte).

In the UK: 150 New Bond Street, London W1YOAQ, tel: 0171-493 3201, fax: 0171-493 9065.

Information office in Clare

In the US: 757 Third Avenue, New York, NY 10017, tel: 212-418 0880, fax: 212-371 9052.

Local tourist offices can make accommodation bookings for a nominal fee. They also supply information on festivals and events, walking and nature trails and local attractions, and have a selection of maps and books for sale. They are usually open Monday to Friday from 9am to 6pm, Saturday 9am to 1pm. Here are the main ones:

Limerick city, Arthur's Quay, tel: 061-317522; fax: 061-317939; **Ennis**, Clare Road, tel: 065-28366; fax: 065-28366; **Shannon Airport**, tel: 061-61664; fax: 061-471664; **Galway city**, 1 Victoria Place, Eyre Square, tel: 091-563081; fax: 091-565201; **Westport**, The Mall, tel: 098-25711; fax: 098-27609; **Sligo**, Áras Reddan, Temple Street, tel: 071-61201; fax: 071-60360.

Accommodation

Riverside B&B, Galway

There is a wide choice of places to stay in the West, ranging from the luxury country house hotel to the simple cottage B&B. It is a good idea, if your budget allows, to vary your kind of accommodation in order to sample at least one 'castle' hotel, as well as a simple, homely B&B. The average B&B costs from about £15 to £25 per person. If you are staying more than one night, the rate is negotiable. There is also a reasonable, if not extensive choice of middle price range hotels, often in very beautiful locations. Because the West is a destination for outdoor lovers, and because the tourist season runs only from April to September or October, hotels do not generally have much in the way of indoor sports facilities. There are some with pools and gyms, but they tend to be the exception.

The Irish Tourist Board tourist information offices listed on page 76 will book a room for a nominal fee. They also have information on self-catering options. Many but by no means all self-catering properties in the West are newly-built, traditional-style cottages grouped together in clusters or holiday villages. If you want an isolated cottage on the side of a mountain, miles from the nearest neighbour, be sure this is what you are getting when you book.

77

Lighthouse B&B on Clare Island

Hotel selection

The following is a selective list of good places to stay, listed according to the categories: ££££ = very expensive (£90 and over per person sharing); £££ = expensive (£60–90 per person sharing); ££ = moderate (£30–£60 per person sharing); £ inexpensive (under £30 per person).

Aran Islands
Mainistir House, Inishmore, tel: 099-61169, fax: 61351. B&Bs abound on the Aran Islands, and you can book a

Mainistir House

room when booking your ferry or flight. This one is something different – a hostel with private double or twin rooms where owner-chef Joël d'Anjou has built up a reputation for imaginative cooking both at breakfast and dinner.

Ballina
Mount Falcon Castle, Co. Mayo, tel: 096-70811, fax: 71517. Legendary hospitality in relaxed surroundings. Private fishing. ££

Ballyvaughan
Gregan's Castle, Co. Clare, tel: 065-77005, fax: 77111. An elegant country house hotel with extensive gardens in the heart of the Burren with breathtaking views over Galway Bay. £££.

Cashel Bay
Cashel House, Co. Galway, tel: 095-31003, fax: 31077. The ultimate Connemara hideaway, elegant and comfortable, and laden with antiques. £££.

Clifden
Erriseask House, Ballyconneely, Co. Galway, tel: 095-23553, fax: 23639. Small modern country hotel set amidst some of Connemara's best coastal scenery with a high reputation for food. £££. **The Quay House**, Co. Galway, tel: 095-21369, fax: 21608. A stylish, characterful country house and restaurant on the edge of town. ££.

Cong
Ashford Castle

Ashford Castle, Cong, Co. Mayo, tel: 092-46003, fax: 46260. American-run castle hotel with high standards of comfort and decor and good sporting facilities. ££££.

Galway City
Ardilaun House Hotel, Taylor's Hill, tel: 091-521433, fax: 521546. Charming old world hotel in quiet, leafy location. £££. **Brennan's Yard Hotel**, Lower Merchant's Road, tel: 056-568166, fax: 568262. Interesting warehouse conversion in city centre. ££. **Adare Guest House**, 5 Father Griffin Place, tel: 091-582638, fax: 583963. Well-located, unpretentious accommodation near city centre. £. **Norman Villa**, 86 Lower Salthill, tel & fax: 091-521131. Victorian townhouse with brass beds and Irish linen. £.

Kinvara
Merriman Inn, Co. Galway, tel: 091-638222, fax: 637686. Large thatched building dating from 1997 in the centre of this attractive fishing village. ££. **Burren View Farmhouse**, Doorus, Co. Galway, tel: 091-37142, fax: 0905-42952. Simple farmhouse with peaceful views. £.

Lahinch
Aberdeen Arms Hotel, Co. Clare, tel: 065-81100, fax: 81228. Attractive Victorian hotel in small seaside golfing village with long sandy beach and dunes. ££.

Leenane
Delphi Lodge, Co. Galway, tel: 095-42211, fax: 42296. Romantic Georgian country house in remote Connemara valley. Lovely lakeside setting, private fly fishing. ££.

Letterfrack
Rosleague Manor Hotel, Co. Galway, tel: 095-41101, fax: 41168. Beautifully situated Georgian country house in scenic Connemara with grounds running down to the sea. £££.

Limerick
Castletroy Park, Dublin Road, tel: 061-335566, fax: 331117. Well-designed modern red brick hotel on the edge of town, with superb leisure facilities. £££. **Jury's Inn**, Lower Mallow Street, Mount Kennett Place, tel: 061-207000, fax: 400966. A large, modern hotel overlooking the Shannon. £.

Lisdoonvarna
Ballinalacken Castle, Co. Clare, tel/fax: 065-74025. A converted shooting lodge on the coast road outside town. Superb views of the Aran islands. ££.

Recess
Ballynahinch Castle Hotel, Ballinafad, Co. Galway, tel: 095-31006, fax: 31085. A historic house full of character, splendidly sited in the wilds of Connemara. Private salmon fishing. £££.

Private fishing at Ballynahinch

Sligo
Ballincar House Hotel, Rosses Point Road, Co. Sligo, tel: 071-45361, fax: 44198. Scenically located modern country house near Sligo town, with excellent restaurant. £££. **Markree Castle**, Collooney, Co. Sligo, tel: 071-67800, fax: 67840. Massive castle with excellent restaurant. £££. **Seaview Farmhouse**, Raghly. Co. Sligo, tel: 071/63640. Comfortable modern bungalow with spectacular sea views and beachside location. £.

Westport
Hotel Westport, Co. Mayo, tel: 098-25122, fax 26739. Comfortable, modern hotel near town centre. Good sports facilities. ££. **Olde Railway Hotel**, The Mall, Co. Mayo, tel: 098-25166, fax 25090. Family-run hotel in town centre, more than 200 years old. ££.

Index